Writing Resource Book

Particular contributors to the *Writing: Resource Book* include:

- Glenda Raison, Education Department of Western Australia,
- Judith Rivalland, Edith Cowan University
- Beverly Derewianka, University of Wollongong
- Terry D Johnson, University of Victoria, British Columbia
- Dr Peter Sloan, Edith Cowan University
- Dr Ross Latham, Edith Cowan University
- Kay Kovalevs, Education Department of Western Australia,
- Ross Bindon, Education Department of Western Australia,
- Kevlynn Annandale, Education Department of Western Australia,
- Judith Larsen, Education Department of Western Australia,
- Alison Dewsbury, Education Department of Western Australia,

First Steps was developed by the Education Department of Western Australia under the direction of Alison Dewsbury.

Rigby Heinemann

Rigby Heinemann
a division of Reed International Books Australia Pty Ltd
22 Salmon Street, Port Melbourne, Victoria 3207
World Wide Web http://www.rigby.heinemann.com.au
Email info@rigby.heinemann.com.au

Offices in Sydney, Brisbane, Perth and Adelaide. Associated
companies, branches and representatives throughout the world.

Published by Rigby Heinemann on behalf of the Education
Department of Western Australia

© Education Department of Western Australia
Previous edition published by AddisonWesley Longman
This edition published by Rigby Heinemann 1997

2001 2000 1999 1998 1997
10 9 8 7 6 5 4 3

Cataloguing-in-publication data

Writing: resource book

ISBN 0 7312 2358 6

1. Creative writing (Primary education). 2. Language arts (Primary).
I. Western Australia. Education Dept. (Series: First Steps
(Perth, W.A.)).

372.623044

Contents

General Introduction

The First Steps *Writing: Resource Book* complements the *Writing: Developmental Continuum* and aims to provide teachers with additional ideas for teaching students how to write texts that will satisfy their social or personal needs. Many of the ideas suggested can be modified for use with children at different developmental phases.

The first two chapters include an overview of general approaches to teaching the complex process of writing in the classroom. They include a brief reference to different approaches to the teaching of writing and offer suggestions about developing a classroom in which writing is seen as something to look forward to.

Each of the following six chapters deals with a different form of writing and includes a description of the form, information about its structure, suggestions for learning experiences that enable students to explore and write the form and assessment ideas. Ideas are suggested to help children understand the purpose for writing, the structure and language features of each form and the processes involved in writing. There are also ideas for planning programs to include a range of written forms.

Where possible the teaching of conventions associated with particular forms of writing are included in the section dealing with that form. However, the chapter entitled 'Teaching Grammar' explores some options for teaching Grammar and provides brief background information for teachers.

The final chapter of the book deals with suggestions for helping children who are reluctant to write or who are having problems with writing.

Throughout the book there is a strong emphasis on the integration of spoken and written language, the need to encourage students to take control of their writing, the need to allow students to reflect on their learning and the need to provide real purposes and audiences for writing.

Chapter 1:

First Steps Writing in the Classroom

Children learn to write and write to learn. In the school environment the focus of teaching should be to provide a variety of real situations that require the use of written language so that children can develop a range of strategies and skills that will enable them to function in society as literate adults. In addition to this, teachers should aim to create a love of writing and an appreciation of its value so that children choose to write.

Approaches to Teaching Writing

There are various schools of thought about teaching writing. The First Steps *Writing: Resource Book* combines a number of ideas to generate a practical approach to teaching writing in schools.

First Steps values the processes that Graves (1981) recommends and also acknowledges the value of the genrist approach (Martin and Rothery 1986, Derewianka 1990 and Dr Peter Sloan and Dr Ross Latham 1990) because of its focus on communicative competence linking the learning of speaking with the learning of writing. This approach also develops the writer's awareness of different forms of text and the registers within those forms. In addition the *First Steps* approach incorporates ideas from Terry D Johnson (1988) who advocates a problem-solving approach to teaching writing. Johnson suggests that a special focus should be placed on the specific purpose and intended audience for the writing and that after writing children should be encouraged to evaluate the effectiveness of their own writing.

Why is a Problem-Solving Approach So Powerful?

This approach can be adapted to teach all forms of writing and it enables children to:

- analyse the structure and organisation of different forms of text
- focus on the language appropriate to the form
- construct their own rules for the writing of different forms of text
- modify and extend their rules in the light of further experience

When children are learning to write a specific text form it is necessary to provide them with structure and guidance. It is important, however, that children are also given sufficient opportunities and time to choose their own topics, purposes and audiences. They need a balance between structure and freedom to experiment with different forms of writing.

Writing for Authentic Purposes

Writing must be introduced in meaningful contexts that enable children to focus on questions such as 'What is my purpose and audience?' rather than 'What shall I write about?' and teachers need to frequently draw children's attention to the formula:

PURPOSE + AUDIENCE = FORM

In this way children can develop and practise their skills in authentic situations where there are audiences other than the teacher.

Children (especially those at risk) need to see that writing is useful to them if they are to fully engage in, and appreciate the process. By using writing to perform specific, clearly defined tasks in meaningful contexts they will see writing as a rewarding activity. They are more likely to remember how to use conventions if they are practising the use of them in their own writing, i.e. embedded in a context that has real meaning.

Many problems encountered by teachers of children's writing can be traced to children's perception that writing has no real or meaningful purpose and no real audience. If a child has no interest in the purpose, form or audience of a piece of writing, no amount of revising, editing or proof reading on the part of the writer will

David M
3 Campsie st,
SHENTON PARK 6008

19th October, 1988

Mr J. R.
Manager
Forest Edge Camp
Waroona 6257

Dear Mr R   ,

I am writing to you concerning the Primary School camp on the 14th November, 1988. I want to know what my child, David McC is going to be doing because I am NOT going to pay fifty dollars for my child to play, eat and sleep. It would cost about ten dollars for him to eat for three days, and it doesn't cost anything for him to play and sleep at home. I would also like to know, is my child going to learn?

What is my child going to do? I am NOT going to pay fifty dollars for my child to be killed falling of a cliff.

Please reply soon.

Yours failhfully,

DM.

(mr)DAVID M
(Parent)

J   R
Forest Edge Camp
Waroona 6257

24th October, 1988

MR D. M
3 Campsie St
Shenton Park 6008

Dear Mr M
unkind letter about the   'I'm repleying to youre Primary School Camp.

You're paying $50 for eating, sleeping, travelling excursions, games, and other things. That would be worth about $75 plus your getting Free drinks and other food. You're not paying $50 for your child playing, eating and sleeping.

I hope your child does fall off the edge of a cliff and die. And I hope that he isn't like you and he is learning.

Yours sincerely

JR

(MR. J   R)

(Camp manager)

2

make the writing effective. In schools it is not always easy to engage children in writing tasks that they see as authentic especially if writing is only done 'on Tuesday mornings', to get a mark out of ten or to copy notes from the blackboard. Therefore it is important for teachers to be explicit about how writing enables us to do things that meet our needs. The specific context will motivate the writing event. For example a year 6/7 class found a letter to the editor about horses allowed to graze in a nearby National Park. Some children strongly disagreed with the contents of the letter and decided to write a reply. They needed access to information that showed how to put an opposing view. The teacher was able to help them analyse similar texts and together they arrived at a framework for their reply (exposition) and also an understanding of the language features appropriate to that form. Once the children had an authentic purpose for writing they were keen to complete the task for their clearly defined audience.

Of course all school writing should be for real purposes and audiences and be connected to reading, talking, listening and the curriculum (real contexts) however sometimes these contexts must be contrived. See the letters at left that were written by children playing the roles of camp manager and parent.

Written language differs from oral language in that the **purpose for writing is generally to communicate over time and or distance**. For instance, if we are not able to remember what to buy at the supermarket we write a list. We write telephone messages so that we can pass them to another person. We write essays so that examiners can ascertain our understanding of a topic without having to ask questions individually and rely on one's ability to recall a number of pieces of information. If we wish to retain information for a period of time then we write. Children need to understand that writing for authentic purposes can help people to communicate information over time and distance.

Writing structure and formats vary according to the purpose and function of the text and readers expect texts to be written in particular ways. We expect that lists are written down the page (because the purpose is to easily mark off items). We expect informational texts to have headings, subheadings, table of contents, index and glossary (so that we can gain easy access to specific information). It would be surprising to find a fairy story written like a list. We expect to read a story from beginning to end, not to mark off items. Children need to read a range different text types and to learn to structure the writing of them so that they can select the form that best suits the purpose and achieves the maximum effect on the audience.

In the classroom it is necessary to provide **a balance between narrative and other forms of writing**. This involves children reading and writing in many content areas where they may be conducting research and presenting a factual report to another group, recording procedure for an experiment in Science for their own future reference, writing a recount of a recent excursion for school assembly, explaining how a phenomena occurred in Social Studies presenting a persuasive argument in Health and so on. There is also a place for developing the reading and writing of a variety of narrative texts to entertain, amuse or extend imagination. In order to provide suitable models of written language teachers need to understand the structure and features of different forms so that they can be explicit about what is required and intervene appropriately as the need arises.

The Role of the Teacher

Teachers are responsible for facilitating children's learning. In order to provide a range of authentic language activities teachers need to be aware of the different ways language is used in different subject areas of the curriculum. It is the teacher who plans and models appropriate forms in context, providing a balance between informational and narrative writing and reading. Teaching plans can be made for whole class, small groups and individuals. As well as planning experiences teachers need to be flexible enough to take advantage of 'teachable moments' as they present themselves. The teacher's role is to observe and support children as their writing develops and to intervene appropriately so that each child can achieve success.

Teacher beliefs about how children learn language will provide the basis for the kinds of learning environment established in classrooms. Although many teachers share common beliefs and philosophies about language learning, no two classrooms will look or sound the same. Individual teachers and children shape the environments to support their own particular needs. Translating beliefs into practice involves teachers in decisions about their own teaching practice and the social environment that they see as the most effective for successful learning.

Planning for Writing

Writing is an amazingly complex activity. The writer is simultaneously involved with thinking of what to write, coherence and cohesion of the text, formation and legibility of individual letters, spelling, grammar including punctuation, layout, tone and register, organisation and selection of appropriate content for an intended audience. It is impossible, even for skilled and talented writers, to control all aspects of writing at once. Children need a clear framework within which they can express and order their ideas, thus reducing the complexity of the task and the demands on their working memory. They also need to be able to focus on one or two aspects at one time so that they can practise new skills until they become automatic. The teacher who demands neat writing, correct punctuation and perfect spelling while children are learning to master new skills runs the risk of promoting the continuation of short boring texts written by children who have no interest in the message only in what the teacher demands. Children cannot manage all the demands of written language concurrently.

Opportunity to interact with the teacher and peers is an essential part of learning to write. Children can be encouraged to question, compare, modify and share with peers throughout the writing process. The talk generated in problem-solving sessions provides crucial information for students about the writing process and also gives teachers an insight into children's understandings.

Time to practise the skills and develop understandings is an essential component of the writing program. Children also need time to reflect on what they know and to think about what they need to know so that they have ownership and control of their own writing development.

Teachers need to plan for optimum learning conditions and may choose to consider the following questions:

How can I plan in advance so that a range of resources including books, magazines, tapes, videos, maps can be collected?

How do I cater for the language opportunities that can be generated as the topic is studied?

Have I collected a range of published books that demonstrate good models of forms of text I wish to teach?

Am I aware of teaching points that may be derived from different texts?

Have I planned opportunities for regular purposeful demonstrations in modelled and shared reading and writing sessions?

Have I planned excursions and notified parents of the topics to be covered?

Where possible, have I integrated language across the curriculum?

Have I ensured that children can use a range of forms for different purposes and audiences?

How can I ensure that there is a balance between narrative and informational writing?

What opportunities am I providing for children to pursue their own personal writing as well as teacher directed activities?

How can I use the content areas of the curriculum (e.g. Social Studies, Science, Health) to further the children's writing and reading of different forms of text?

Have I identified the major skills and understandings to be developed within the unit of work, e.g. gathering and organising information about an animal, describing how humans modify their environment, arguing to conserve a non-renewable resource, writing a fairy tale?

Have I allowed enough flexibility for children to negotiate some aspects of the topic?

Am I communicating to parents on a regular basis so that they understand the type of program that is being delivered at school?

Have I considered the school policy and school planning so that they are reflected in my program?

Planning for writing in all areas of the curriculum will help ensure that it happens in meaningful contexts.

The Classroom Environment

Teachers are largely responsible for creating a climate that is supportive and positive. The classroom needs to be a place where children are secure in the knowledge that their efforts are valued and problem solving is encouraged. There must be time for children to reflect on their learning, to represent it in a way that is meaningful to them and to report to others what they learned.

The following questions are included to help teachers reflect on their contribution to a desirable classroom climate:

Do I believe that all children can learn to write?

How do I show that I am a caring teacher who understands that all children need to experience success as they engage in learning activities?

How can I act as facilitator and co-learner (rather than the source of all knowledge)?

Am I providing a balance between teacher-designed activities and uninterrupted blocks of time where children can pursue their interests and have direct access to the stimulating environment?

Am I always aware of the children's self esteem and self image?

How do I cater for whole class, small group and individual needs?

What activities am I providing that enable children to engage at their phase of development?

How am I helping children to progress and develop their abilities beyond their current capabilities?

How do I show that I am continually evaluating, modifying and changing practices according to the changing literacy demands?

How do I make explicit the links between reading, writing, speaking and listening as I integrate all elements of language across curriculum areas?

Do I provide frequent demonstrations of what real readers and writers do?

Am I providing models of processes and products through a range of different activities?

Do I observe children and assess their language development in the context of the classroom?

Do I give immediate and suitable feedback?

Do I provide opportunities for other meaningful feedback? (Sharing times at the end of sessions, individual, partner or group conferences and discussions.) These times are useful for all students but especially those who have difficulty writing from a reader's perspective and choosing relevant details for a particular audience.

How do the children demonstrate that they are problem solvers and risk takers?

Are the children becoming independent learners?

Do the children set and review personal goals and engage in the evaluation of their own progress?

Do the children cooperate and work collaboratively?

Do children participate in making classroom rules?

Are children aware of class routines and time commitments?

Do the children have the opportunities to use literacy for their own authentic and meaningful purposes?

Are the children able to engage in spontaneous child-initiated activities ?

Do the children understand what they are learning, why they are learning and how they are learning?

Do children take time to reflect, represent and report their new knowledge or understandings?

Physical Layout and Resources

The classroom needs to be organised so that teachers can provide whole class, small group and individual teaching and so that children have access to resources. A print rich environment that is meaningful and useful will encourage children and teachers to take full advantage of opportunities to focus on particular aspects of language. The physical layout and available resources need to be conducive to learning.

Is the classroom organised so that whole class, small group, and individual activities can be conducted effectively?

Is there a large area to accommodate the whole class?

Are children's desks clustered so that groups of four or six children can work collaboratively?

Is there an easel and/or board in the area where modelled and shared reading and writing sessions are conducted?

Is there storage that is accessible to children?

Is the classroom a functioning literacy environment that has interesting things to read and write about?

Are there books and other suitable texts in close proximity to various settings?

Are there writing implements and materials in the vicinity of, and relevant to, the interesting things in the classroom e.g. music books near the piano, information books near the pet house, weather books, TV schedule and newspapers near the weather chart, atlases, road maps, street directories near the 'Our Community' display?

Are there enough suitable resources accessible to the children to foster independent learning e.g. a range of different types of dictionaries, thesauruses, reference material, listening posts, tape recorders, computers, videos, atlases?

Is there a range of different texts both fiction and non-fiction?

Are the visible references where they are needed, clear, at the child's eye level and current?

Are the print displays in the room likely to capture children's attention and support and stimulate literacy e.g. reference charts for class routines or rosters, charts about print conventions, 'How to ...' directions for activities, alphabet friezes, words lists, catalogues, cookbooks, local newspapers, functional labels?

Are there current child-generated messages, captions, articles, reports, stories, instructions?

Are there child- and teacher-made books that reflect a range of shared language experiences?

Is there display space for children's own work?

Planning the Language Session

Reading, writing, speaking and listening are all interrelated so it is not necessary to try and separate them as fragmented areas. The language session is more effective if large blocks of time are allocated to allow opportunities for language learning. Teachers also need to be flexible in their approach so that they capitalise on children's interests.

The following elements could be included in most language sessions:

Shared reading
This whole class activity may include opportunities to set the scene, introduce a topic, continue a serial or introduce a new form of text. The focus will vary.

Silent reading
The whole class (including the teacher) read from texts they have selected. It is a quiet non-pressured time where everyone participates at their own level.

Reading mini lessons or demonstrations
These short lessons for the whole class may focus on
- a strategy, e.g. what to do if you don't know a word,
- a skill or understanding, e.g. what is a glossary?
- a classroom procedure, e.g. how to prepare for a reading conference.

Reading activities
Class may work in groups or individually on a pre-set task or an elective task depending on the purpose for the lesson. During this time the teacher works with small groups of children to consolidate particular aspects of their reading. Groups are chosen according to need and vary from day to day. Reading conferences can also be planned for this time.

Sharing time
Children share with whole class or in small groups and are given time to reflect on their learning and to gain insights into others' learning. This is a critical aspect of learning.

Writing mini lessons or demonstrations
These short lessons for the whole class may focus on
- a strategy, e.g. how to use a framework to plan a written text,
- a skill or understanding, e.g. What is a paragraph?
- a classroom procedure, e.g. how make entries in a writing log.

Writing time
Class may work in groups or individually on a pre-set task or an elective task depending on the purpose for the lesson. During this time the teacher works with small groups of children to consolidate particular aspects of their writing. Groups are chosen according to need and vary from day to day. Writing conferences can also be planned for this time.

Sharing time
Sharing time provides real audience responses and opportunities for interaction and reflection. Classes can participate in whole class sharing but this sometimes becomes tedious so small group sharing is probably more beneficial.

Spelling and word study
Time is set aside for children to explore words and to learn words which they need in their writing. During this time children may be selecting words to enter in their personal word lists (from their writing or have-a-go pads), learning personal words,

partner testing, making entries in their spelling logs, or exploring words using selected activities such as 'Word Sorts', 'Secret Messages' and 'What Comes Next?'. The teacher can work with groups of children during this time.

The outline on pages 11–12 shows how one teacher incorporates these ideas over a week. Times vary according to outside timetable demands.

Focus: Our Environment

Monday	Tuesday	Wednesday	Thursday	Friday
Mathematics **8.45**				

Language session

10.00 Shared reading (whole class)

Shared reading Introduce topic.	Read letter about horses in National Parks.	Read other fiction or non fiction texts that focus on the environment.		

10.15

Sustained silent reading (whole class)

Students choose from range of resources in Environment Corner.

10.30 Recess

10.45 Reading mini lesson or demonstration (whole class)

Title—Discuss things that affect our environment. Demonstrate skimming and scanning techniques using a newspaper article.	List interesting words children have found in their reading. Use context clues to find meanings. What other resources will help?	Analyse four texts about horses in National Parks to establish how written arguments are constructed.	Look at the way authors position readers by the careful use of emotive language.	Content words using context clues. Interesting Words Chart.

11.00 Reading activities—small groups, mixed ability

Search through newspapers to find articles, letters etc. about the environment.	Share articles with other groups and decide on aspects to pursue.	Organise children into roles of rangers, horse owners, non horse owners and conservationists. Each group discusses and makes notes about the topic from their viewpoint. Groups then re-form so that each group has one of each role. Individuals put their point of view and others ask questions.

Each day different children are chosen (according to need) for Instructional Group Focuses in D.S.R. Reading strategies to be used this week: what to do if you don't know a word, oral summaries, skimming and scanning.

11.25 Sharing time (Whole class sharing in small groups)

Monday	Tuesday	Wednesday	Thursday	Friday
11.35 Writing mini lesson or demonstration (whole class)				
Brainstorm all you know about the environment. Categorise information into a structured overview of topic. Place in view of children.	Model how to write notes and summaries. Revise how to use suggested headings to organise information.	Model use of 'Exposition Rules' to plan writing.	Model writing a short written argument using information from earlier analysis of 'Horses in National Parks' texts.	Model proof-reading and editing strategies using yesterday's modelled text.

11.50 Writing activities

Children involved in:
Writing notes and preparing letters to the editor about 'Horses in National Parks'.
(They chose this aspect to pursue first. They decided their position on the topic and planned their letters accordingly.)
Completing writing log.
Making entries in journal.

Small group and individual conferences are conducted as required throughout the week.

Lunch

12.45 Resume above program.

1.20 Sharing time. Writing so far—whole class in small groups.

1.35 Spelling and word study (whole class, group and individual)

Routine varies to include the following areas:
Words are taken from children's writing and class topic words.
Instruction time for whole class needs.
Entry of suitable words from have-a-go pads and written work in all areas.
Learning personal words for partner test (journal).
Partner tests.
Group or individual activities, directed or open, to focus on particular areas of need.
Individual or small group conferences with teacher.
Setting goals for spelling.
Spelling log.

Chapter 2:

Exploring Different Forms of Writing

Introducing Forms of Writing

The writing process is graphically represented below.

CONTEXT (PURPOSE + AUDIENCE)

Internal or external stimulus → **TRIGGERS** A social or personal purpose for writing, i.e., to communicate meaning to another person or self

DETERMINES →

STRUCTURE (FORM OF TEXT)

Selection of the form of text to meet the social or personal purpose.

↓

Construction of the text framework or stages which relate to the selected form of text.

PUBLICATION

Text is refined, edited and proofed to make it technically correct in relation to the purpose.

COMPOSITION

Ideas are written using shared conventions and appropriate forms

Ideas/data are generated to fit the parts of the framework.

FACILITATES

The process of writing is set in motion when a writer recognises a need or purpose for writing a text. In order to achieve the purpose and satisfy the need, one form of text will be superior to all others. Thus, the next step in the writing process is the identification of the form of text that best matches the writer's purpose.

Each text form discussed in this resource book is characterised by a distinctive structure. The next step, therefore, in the writing process, is the identification of the framework that the writer will use to guide the writing of the text.

The purpose of writing a text is to convey ideas or data to another person or to record information for subsequent personal perusal, study, pleasure, etc. The next step in the writing process is to generate the ideas and content matter that fit the parts of the framework of the selected text form. The writing process now requires the writer to apply writing skills to the data or ideas to produce them as meaningful sentences that go well together to make coherent paragraphs. Paragraphs are linked logically to form a cohesive text.

The final steps in the process involve the writer's technical and editing skills. By means of these, the writer ensures that the text is technically correct so that it can successfully achieve his/her original purpose for writing. (Sloan and Latham)

So that teachers can choose an approach that supports their beliefs about writing, a number of sample texts have been included in this book. The texts included for each form (pages 23, 47, 70, 87, 113, and 131) are drawn from children in various schools and have been trialled as texts to be analysed by other classes. The spelling has been corrected and they have been typed. They are meant to provide a starting resource. Teachers will, of course, build a bank of their own samples from children's writing so that contexts are more meaningful. There are many other samples of children's writing included in this book.

Children operating in the Role Play or Experimental Phases need a special approach to learning to write because they are largely self-centred and are coming to terms with a wide variety of concepts and conventions of print as well as coping with the physical and cognitive demands of putting their ideas on paper.

Children who are just beginning to make marks on paper and 'write' for themselves need:

- many opportunities to write freely
- to see demonstrations of how others use writing
- to choose their own topics and forms
- to be able to write in a supportive environment where they can experiment and take risks in the knowledge that their efforts and approximations are accepted and praised
- teachers and other significant adults who can reassure writers that what they are doing is wonderful
- supportive comments that focus on the message in the child's writing rather than correct spelling, neat handwriting or other technical aspects
- models of significant adults using the writing process in a variety of forms to show children how writing works. Just by 'thinking aloud' when doing such tasks as filling in a bank form, writing a shopping list or message, adults can model how they use writing to transact their daily business

Students operating in the Early, Conventional and Proficient Phases of writing need:

- opportunities to use a recursive revision process (Graves 1981); that is, to write, read, reread, and rewrite continually while producing their writing
- to be given explicit guidance in using a range of forms of text
- to be shown how to analyse models of the appropriate forms and create their own set of 'rules' for writing. (wherever possible the models should be of children's work)
- to be encouraged to evaluate their own work using their set of 'rules' and then to modify these rules according to changed perceptions after writing (Johnson 1988)
- to have an immediate and personal audience other than the teacher
- to understand that **purpose + audience = form**. Once students know who they are writing for and why, the form the writing must take becomes obvious.

What Can Be Taught?

Various strategies can be used to teach children information about writing. Writers need to know about processes such as planning and drafting, particular elements or conventions of writing and how to structure a variety of forms of writing. Below are some elements that could be effectively introduced, consolidated or revised as required by the writer.

Processes of Writing	*Forms of Writing*	*Conventions and Skills of Writing*
• Topic selection • Selection of appropriate content • Planning and organising • Researching • Asking for help • Drafting • Altering text • Proof reading • Checking spelling • Sharing • Conferencing	• Recounts • Descriptions • Reports • Summaries • Instructions • Letters • Invitations • Figures • Maps • Advertisements • Timetables • Narrative forms • Poetic forms	• Directionality—left to right, top to bottom • Spaces between words • Sentence structure • Spelling • Sentence manipulation and modification • Vocabulary use • Grammar

Children need to be taught different written forms, processes and conventions in context, across all curriculum areas at both primary and secondary levels.

While approaches to writing are specifically mentioned in this book the following components can be integrated and incorporated into various aspects of the school language program emphasising the link between reading, writing, speaking and listening.

A balanced program includes:

Shared reading of texts which are exemplars of the form to be taught. Children read with the teacher and discuss the purposes for the use of the form in our society, the type of content presented, the structure of the texts and function of each part and the type of language used.

Guided reading of models of text forms. Teacher can use gentle guidance and questioning to encourage children to discover the text features for themselves. In this book there are a number of sample texts (see pages 56, 75, 95–6 and 136 as examples) that could be used to focus children's attention on the textual features of different forms so that they can problem solve to construct guidelines for writing each form.

Modelled writing is a powerful strategy that can be used to demonstrate a range of skills processes and strategies. In primary schools modelled writing is a daily event that enables teachers to share with children the procedures of writing.

What Can Be Modelled?

Teachers can:

Model writing by 'thinking aloud' to show how writers make a decisions about such things as:

- what to write
- how to start
- how to revise and edit writing
- how to choose information which is relevant to the audience
- how to present information and ideas
- use of word banks, wall charts and other classroom references
- how to experiment with writing
- how to write a new form of text.

After modelling it is important to reiterate the main teaching points:

> *'I feel really happy with this summary. Now let's list the main things I've included—a title, the main idea, the supporting information, a concluding sentence. Yes, I think that's all. Can anyone think of anything else that should be included?'*

This gives children a clear reference point for their own writing. It also provides a focus for future writing conferences.

Why Model Writing?

Modelled writing gives children the opportunity to see the processes through which writers work. As teachers illustrate procedures through modelling, children see that writing is an interactive process; they are reassured that writers 'make mistakes'; they become aware of the processes of editing; and they develop confidence in using the processes themselves.

The purpose of modelling may vary according to the form or conventions being modelled. Teachers can incorporate a range of teaching points in each session. In this way, children have the opportunity to see that all aspects of writing are important; that it is important to plan before writing; to edit and proof read; to aim for conventional spelling and syntax; to develop ideas; and that each of these facets of writing contributes to the quality of the meaning conveyed.

Modelled writing provides opportunities to demonstrate to children that the teacher is working with them rather than judging them.

Modelled writing can also be used to teach a particular element in language. For example, if a number of children were beginning to use speech marks, then it would be appropriate for the teacher to model a piece of writing using speech marks and talk about where they go and why. If some children were writing short, repetitive sentences that tended to begin with 'Then', it would be useful to model sentence-combining techniques.

Before writing independently it is often useful for students to participate in the **shared writing** of a text in the new form. It is useful for the teacher to scribe for the children in the first instance and if further practice is required children can be guided to jointly construct a text having seen an adult model the process.

Shared writing can begin with gathering and pooling information about the topic. This may involve demonstrations of how to find information and how to take notes in a way that will suit the composition required for the form. The next step could be to check the structure of the form and organise notes into that structure. The teacher then writes from the notes transforming notes into sentences. Children are encouraged to contribute their ideas as the teacher scribes. Copies of the shared writing may be displayed and used as a reference in the future.

Some teachers find **guided writing** of the new form by the students a worthwhile interim step before students are asked to write independently. Students compose their writing with a partner or in a small group so that there is peer support as they write using the framework demonstrated by the teacher. The teacher's role is to guide and encourage students by giving explicit feedback that refers to the structural or language features required in the text form.

Having been exposed to many examples of the new form, children now move to **independent construction** of a text using the form with a related topic. Each child chooses a topic and writes a draft using the framework and examples from the previous session.

For example in a year six class where they had looked at expositions dealing with aspects of conservation, several students chose to write to the local newspaper arguing the case for the exclusion of horses from a nearby National Park. Other students wrote to the local government authority to put a case for a tree planting program. Several students chose to write to manufacturers to argue the case for environmentally friendly packaging. All students used the exposition form.

After completing their drafts children are encouraged to refer to charts, exemplars and other reference material to evaluate their control of the form of writing and whether the purpose was achieved. They can also set goals for improvement. Children then confer with peers or teacher and revise their writing to prepare their texts for publication if required.

Assessment and Evaluation of Writing

The Teacher

Assessment and evaluation of writing is an ongoing and integral part of the language program. The First Steps *Writing: Developmental Continuum* provides a broad view of children's general writing progress. In this *Resource Book* there is a continuum of development for each form of writing. These continua have been developed over a number of years from samples of children's writing collected after they have been exposed to a form. They rely on teacher observation of children's writing behaviours and the collection of children's written work. They are probably suitable for use once children have reached the *Early Writing Phase* of the *Writing: Developmental Continuum*.

Teachers may use these continua to evaluate children's control over the features of each particular form and to direct their teaching of the form.

Children may exhibit indicators in more than one phase and their control of the form may fluctuate according to the complexity of the topic content involved, e.g. they may show good control over procedure writing when writing a recipe but their control may not be so good when they are trying to record a complex science experiment using technical terms.

Samples of the combined use of the *Writing: Developmental Continuum* and the continuum for each form of writing are included towards the end of each chapter to show how teachers use a combination of both to evaluate children's writing. It is recommended that at least three samples of writing be collected before attempting to make evaluations.

The Student

Students can be directly involved in keeping records of their writing progress.

Writing logs can be established so that when children are writing they record the date, form of writing, intended audience and whether or not the writing is completed. Children need to be given time to update their logs and to be shown that all writing is to be entered.

Students can set and review writing goals. (The checklists included at the end of each chapter in this book could provide the basis for students' own goal setting.) The 'Things I Can Do' pages from the *Writing: Developmental Continuum* may also provide ideas for goal setting.

Periodically students can be asked to reflect on their writing progress in conferences or by writing responses in their writing journals, e.g. Me as a Writer, What I Know About Writing Narratives. These responses will help students clarify their understandings and give teachers valuable insights.

Overview of Major Forms of Writing

The forms of writing selected for this book are generally considered to be those often required in primary and secondary school settings. Each form of writing includes explanation of the form and suggested contexts for its use, followed by a description of the framework and language features that are typical of that form. There is also a range of activities that will help children understand and use the form being introduced. These activities include oral language suggestions, modelled and shared reading and writing activities, and individual reading and writing that may be used to consolidate and extend children's understanding and control of that form of writing. Finally there are ideas for children's self-assessment and a continuum of indicators that may be use by teachers to assess children's progress and to formulate future teaching objectives and plans. There are samples of children's writing included to help teachers use the continuum.

There are many forms of writing. The following are elaborated in this book.

NARRATIVES
RECOUNTS
PROCEDURES
REPORTS
EXPLANATIONS
EXPOSITIONS

OVERVIEW OF MAJOR FORMS

CONTEXTS (EXAMPLES OF PURPOSES AND AUDIENCE)		FORMS	LANGUAGE FEATURES
NARRATIVE	English: Write a story, fable, myth, fairytale, poem, or a play History: A historical biography	Purpose: to entertain Focus: sequential specific events Framework: • orientation • initiating events • complications/problems • resolution (may be repeated in episodes)	• defined characters • descriptive language • dialogue • usually past tense
RECOUNT	English: Newspaper account, letters or journals Social Studies: Diary of Captain Cook Maths: How I solved the problem Health: Record of exercise and food for the day Science: Recount of chickens hatching	Purpose: to retell events Focus: sequential specific events Framework: • orientation • events in time-order • re-orientation (optional) • evaluation (optional)	• specific participants • linking words to do with time, e.g. later, after, before • action verbs • simple past tense
PROCEDURE	English: An instruction manual Social Studies: How to read a map Maths: How to find the perimeter using concrete material Health: Recipe for health cookies Science: Writing up an experiment	Purpose: to deal with the way to do things Focus: sequential general events Framework: • goal • materials • method • evaluation (optional)	• detailed factual description • reader referred to in a general way or not mentioned at all, e.g. draw a line • linking words to do with time, e.g. after, when, as soon as • tense is timeless
REPORT	English: Write a report on life in the 1920's, after reading My Place Social Studies: A report on deserts Health: A report on heart disease Science: A report on birds	Purpose: to classify and describe a class of things Focus: general things Framework: • generalisation/classification • description • summary (optional)	• generalised participants • impersonal objective language • timeless present tense • subject specific vocabulary
EXPLANATION	Social Studies: Explain how soil erosion occurs Explain how seasons occur Health: Explain digestion Science: Explain how rain forms	Purpose: to explain phenomena Focus: general processes Framework: • phenomenon • explanation sequence	• generalised non-human participants • cause and effect relationships • some passives, e.g. is driven by... • timeless present tense, e.g. soil is deposited...
EXPOSITION	English: Does television promote crime in our community? Social Studies: Do you think punishment for crimes in our society is appropriate? Health: Smoking — Is it dangerous? Science: Electricity and magnetism are closely related	Purpose: to argue or persuade Focus: a thesis presented from a particular point of view Framework: • thesis • argument • reiteration	• generalised participants • passives to help text structure • linking words associated with reasoning, e.g. therefore • nominalisation (actions become things), e.g. to pollute becomes pollution

20

Chapter 3:

Narrative

A narrative text tells an imaginative story, although some narratives may be based on facts. Narratives are written in many different forms and each form has distinctive characteristics.

Features of Narratives

Purpose

The main purpose of a narrative is to entertain and engage the reader in an imaginative experience. Some narratives also have other purposes, e.g. they may seek to explain a phenomenon (myths and legends) or to teach a lesson (fables).

Focus

The focus is specific sequential events and actions.

Types

Folktales, fairytales, fables, myths, legends, science fiction, modern fantasy, short stories, picture-story books and ballads are all narrative texts. In this book narrative is dealt with in a generic way, although it is acknowledged that each form of narrative has unique features in addition to the generic structure, e.g. fables include a moral and have animals with human characteristics, picture-story books have 32 pages, fairy tales often have sets of three events, three characters or things etc. Teachers will, of course, adapt the information to the particular form of narrative being investigated.

Contexts for Narrative Writing

Different curriculum areas can be used as a stimulus for story writing, e.g.

English	Stories, plays, fables, myths, legends, ballads, short stories, etc.
Social Studies	An imaginative story based on historical facts, a play about a social problem
Health	Passive Emotions—the story of a smoker
Science	Life in the Pond—the story of frogs threatened by the urban sprawl

Text Organisation

Narratives generally include an *Orientation* in which the setting, time, main character, and possibly some minor characters, of the story are established. This part sets the mood, and invites the reader to continue reading. Details that will be significant later in the story are often included in the orientation.

An event or series of **Events** involving the main character then unfold and lead to a **Complication** in which the character is involved in some conflict. There are often minor conflicts that serve to frustrate or hamper the main character from reaching an ambition or wish. These conflicts serve to build tension and hold the reader's interest as they lead to a major problem or climax.

The complication is resolved satisfactorily in the **Resolution** and loose ends are generally tidied up. Some narratives leave the reader to decide on the ending or resolution while others fill in all details.

Language Features

- Specific, often individual, participants with defined identities. Major participants are human, or sometimes animals with human characteristics
- Mainly action verbs (material processes) but also many verbs that refer to what the human participants said, or felt, or thought (verbal and mental processes)
- Normal past tense
- Many linking words to do with time
- Dialogue often included, during which the tense may change to the present or future
- Descriptive language chosen to enhance and develop the story by creating images in the reader's mind
- Can be written in the first person (I, we) or third person (he, she, they). (In choose-your-own-adventures, the reader is involved in the story as a major character and addressed as 'you')

(Adapted from Derewianka B. 1990, *Exploring How Texts Work*, p. 42.)

Examples

Myths, legends, fables, science fiction, historical fiction, etc.

NARRATIVE

The First Boomerang

One day, manny years ago, there lived
an*t* aboriginal carpenter named Hesaw. He
was well respected by his tribe and was
noted for his creative sculptures. For many
years he had carved creatures from the
local jarrah trees.

As he sat in the warm *spring* sun a sleepy
snake slithered by. Hesaw decided to
carve a snake. Slowly he got up to
find the right piece of wood. When
he was satisfied with his selection
he began to whittle away with his
best blade. The wood was hard
and the carving slow. Hesaw began
to get drowsy. His head nodded and
he fell asleep.

When he awoke the snake he'd
carved looked quite strange. It
seemed bent in the middle and
thin at both ends. Hesaw bent
down and picked up the carved
wood. He threw it as far as he
could — it was of no use he would
start again.

The snake spun through *it*
the air. Hesaw peered as ~~the stick~~
spun around, turned in the air
and came skipping across the
sandy ground at his feet. He
threw it again as hard as he could.
Back came the snake. Hesaw's face began
to split~~,~~ He smiled. He laughed. Tears
flowed down his shining cheeks. He threw
his wonderful snake again and again.
Hesaw had made the first boomerang.

NARRATIVE

- **Orientation**
  - Who, When, Where.

- **Events Which Lead to a Complication or Problem**
  - Includes details which will enhance the later development of the story.
  - Complication involves main characters and generally mirrors complications of real life.
  - There may also be minor complications.

- **Resolution**
  - Complications are resolved in a satisfying manner.

Narrative Framework

The First Boomerang
by Jason P

Orientation	One day, many years ago, there lived an aboriginal carpenter named Hesaw. He was well respected by his tribe and was noted for his creative sculptures. For many years he had carved creatures from the local jarrah trees.	Past tense
	As he sat in the warm spring sunshine a sleepy snake slithered by. Hesaw decided to carve a snake. Slowly he got up to find the right piece of wood. When he was satified with his selection he began to whittle away with his best blade. The wood was hard and the carving slow. Hesaw began to get drowsy. His head nodded and he fell asleep.	Descriptive language to create images
Complication	When he awoke the snake he'd carved looked quite strange. It seemed bent in the middle and thin at both ends. Hesaw bent down and picked up the the carved wood. He threw it as far as he could—it was of no use. He would start again.	Linking words to do with time
	The snake spun through the air. Hesaw peered as it spun around, turned in the air and came skipping across the sandy ground at his feet. He threw it again as hard as he could. Back came the snake. Hesaw's face began to split. He smiled. He laughed. Tears ran down his shining cheeks. He threw his wonderful snake again and again.	Variation in sentence length to provide change of mood and pace.
Resolution	Hesaw had made the first boomerang	

The First Boomerang

by Jason P

One day, many years ago, there lived an aboriginal carpenter named Hesaw. He was well respected by his tribe and was noted for his creative sculptures. For many years he had carved creatures from the local jarrah trees.

As he sat in the warm spring sunshine a sleepy snake slithered by. Hesaw decided to carve a snake. Slowly he got up to find the right piece of wood. When he was satified with his selection he began to whittle away with his best blade. The wood was hard and the carving slow. Hesaw began to get drowsy. His head nodded and he fell asleep.

When he awoke the snake he'd carved looked quite strange. It seemed bent in the middle and thin at both ends. Hesaw bent down and picked up the the carved wood. He threw it as far as he could — it was of no use. He would start again.

The snake spun through the air. Hesaw peered as it spun around, turned in the air and came skipping across the sandy ground at his feet. He threw it again as hard as he could. Back came the snake. Hesaw's face began to split. He smiled. He laughed. Tears ran down his shining cheeks. He threw his wonderful snake again and again.

Hesaw had made the first boomerang

This simple text uses a recognisable Narrative framework and may be used by teachers to introduce and analyse the features of a Narrative.

Exploring and Planning Narratives

All writers need to see how authors compose their stories and need to be exposed to a range of different stories by different authors. They need to be read to, and to have quality texts available for them to read independently. They also need opportunities to talk about stories, to critically evaluate how real authors achieve their purpose and to tell and retell stories. Time to reflect on, and respond to texts is critical to the development of writing.

Activities

Role Play, Experimental and Early Phase writers need to be exposed to a range of stories so that they can begin to write their own. They also need opportunities to talk about stories, to tell and retell familiar stories and to have quality texts available for them to read independently. In addition, they need to be encouraged to have-a-go at writing their own stories and sharing them with others. Children in Conventional and Proficient writing phases need the opportunity to study the craft of authors so that they can see the devices used and how aspects of stories unfold. They need many opportunities to read as writers.

The following activities can be adapted to suit different needs of writers.

Oral activities:
Modelled stories
Story reconstruction
Story makers
Story character interviews
Story telling

Linking reading to writing:
Shared reading
Retell
Story ladder
Literary letters
Map a story
Cause and effect
Text innovation
Change the form
Story grammar

Journals
Descriptions
Picture clues
Character questions

Guiding questions

Character profiles

Complications

Pass it on

Improving children's narrative writing
Sentence manipulation

Word study
Using direct speech
Planning sheets

Oral Activities

Teachers include many activities to develop narrative language in the classroom. The following oral strategies are designed to be integrated or modified to link with existing reading and writing programs. They do not focus on story telling as a performance skill but explore slightly different aspects of narrative, using activities that promote interaction and discussion.

Modelled stories

The modelled story strategy is a hands-on technique that exploits children's love of play materials. It is designed for small groups of pre-primary children but also benefits older children who have had limited contact with story language and structure.

Using story props such as dolls, toy cars, toy animals or a magnetic board and characters the teacher models a story with conventional features, e.g.

Orientation	'Once there was a tiny girl who lived near an old…'
Complication	'She was startled by a…'
Resolution	'…and ran home to safety'
Story language	'Suddenly, a tiny, tiny…, faster and faster, she roared.

Children are invited to help create the story by offering suggestions. Children are then invited to take the storyteller's spot and retell the story using story props or to tell another story. Story props are then left in an accessible part of the classroom for free play activities. If required, the teacher can translate oral stories to written text as a way of showing how writing can record children's thoughts and words for later.

Story reconstruction

The story reconstruction activity is a modification of text reconstruction. The strategy uses oral language to develop understandings about story construction as students analyse pictures, sequence them and then tell the story from the pictures.

Using multiple sets of picture sequences from fairy tales or other known stories, organise children into small groups with as many children as there are pictures in the sequence.

Children sit in circles and each child is assigned a number. Pictures are placed in the middle of the circle. The first person selects and describes the picture that goes first. If the group agrees, the next person has a turn. If not, children discuss this part of the story and reach consensus. Children continue in turn until all pictures are in a logical sequence. Children then retell the story around the circle.

A more complex version of this activity can be made using pictures from an unknown text. Using multiple sets of picture sequences (about four per set) one picture is given to each pair of children. Each pair is then asked to imagine what might have happened before and/or after their picture. The pictures are then discussed by the class and a correct sequence agreed to. The story is then retold from the pictures.

Discussion is important throughout these activities as it gives children an opportunity to substantiate or modify their predictions and to use story language while gaining understanding of story structure.

If required, teachers can write the stories or make story maps of the stories reconstructed.

Story makers
Use different colours to make sets of cards for each element of a story, e.g. pink cards for characters, yellow cards for settings, green cards for problems or complications.

Children work in groups of three and select a card from each category. They jointly compose a story using the information on the cards and then tell the story to another group.

Story character interviews
Story character interviews incorporate shared book and drama techniques. They can provide children with information about how authors construct characters and position readers to infer certain things about characters.

After sharing a story with children ask them to choose their favourite part. Display the book at this page and discuss the events and characters illustrated.

Choose a person to role play one of the characters. Brainstorm possible questions that children would like to ask the character. Choose five children to be the interviewers. They take turns to ask questions of the character. The interviewee can answer creatively by elaborating answers and interviewers can be encouraged to ask follow-up questions. The activity can be repeated using different characters or other parts of the story.

Interviews could be followed by re-telling the story from another character's point of view (orally or in writing).

Story telling
Encourage children to tell their stories to one another before writing.

Linking Reading and Writing

Shared reading
Teachers need to encourage children to see themselves as writers so, when sharing reading, use opportunities to invite children to read critically by examining techniques authors have used. Talk about the way the author has introduced the story and what elements are included. Discuss the complication and resolution. Ask children to try and predict why certain things are mentioned and if they will have significance. Try some of the following questions as you read together.

How does the period in which the story was written affect the story?
How does the author give us information about the main character?
What is actually described and what do we infer?
Why do you think the author included that particular detail or event?
How does this event or detail fit in with the other events or details?
What is the author preparing us for?
What am I learning about this character?
If you were the author what would you make happen?
How did the author tell us about the character?

Who is telling the story? Why is the author telling it from that point of view?
Would the story be any different if it was told from another point of view?
How is the complication introduced?
Could you predict the complication from the clues left by the author?
Are there minor crises that lead to a major problem?
Was the complication resolved in a satisfactory way?
Was the resolution predictable, boring or something unexpected?

By exploring the ways in which different authors use and manipulate narrative structure children internalise the structures and the language used. If they are given many opportunities to discuss the features of a range of texts they are likely to achieve more success when writing narrative texts.

After reading, teachers may like to try some of the following ideas to help students focus on the strategies used by authors to achieve their purposes.

Retell
After children have read or heard a story a number of times ask them to retell it to a friend. Retelling can be written or oral and has many advantages. It helps children internalise the language and structure of narratives and if time is allowed for children to compare and discuss their retells they will also have improved understanding of the story. Written retells give children task practice using writing conventions without the added burden of having to invent a plot. This is especially useful for Early Phase writers who sometimes have difficulty juggling the complex demands of writing.

Story ladder
After reading a story, divide class into groups of 4-6 children. Each group lists the main events in the story deleting the last part of each sentence. Groups swap their list with another group and try to complete each sentence from other group's list.

Literary letters
Children choose a story character and write a letter to that character. They swap their letter with a friend who has to write a reply as the character.

Map a story

GOLDILOCKS o o o o o   THE THREE BEARS x x x x x

Drawing a map that captures events in a story is a useful way of summarising information. Some stories lend themselves to this strategy more than others. Children require several demonstrations of the process before being asked to complete the task independently.

Model how to draw a map that captures the events in a story. The map should show the important events and different settings in the story. After several demonstrations of story mapping ask children to work in groups to make a map. Children can also make individual story maps and retell a story using their story map.

Change the form

Students work in small groups or individually to rewrite a story in a different form, e.g. a comic strip, a play or a picture book.

Cause and effect
After reading and discussing the story, record the main events or episodes and show how actions result in reactions as the plot develops.

Setting	Episode 1	Episode 2	Episode 3, etc.
Who	Goldilocks	Goldilocks	Goldilocks + bears
Where	Bears' house	Bears' house	Bears' house
When			
What	went in	sat on	went to sleep
Initiating event or problem	ate porridge	sat on chairs	bears angry
Reaction	didn't like father's or mother's porridge	didn't like father's or mother's chair	bears angry
Resolution or outcome	ate baby's porridge	broke baby bear's chair	chased Goldilocks

Text innovation
Short texts that feature rhyme, rhythm and repetition are particularly suitable for text innovation activities. After reading a text a number of times children work in groups or individually to write an innovation that changes some aspects of the story but retains the rhythm or rhyme of the original text.

Story grammar

After reading a story, work with children to make a Story grammar.

Teachers and students brainstorm to compile headings that suit the text being read. Children select details from the story and place them under appropriate headings.

Journals

Journals can be used by children as they read independently or after shared reading sessions. The use of journals helps children reflect on the craft of authors. Writing in journals can include questions children have of the text, predictions about what might happen or questions they want to ask during readers' sharing time.

Teachers can model the sorts of questions they may wish to have answered so that students see how authors choose to include things that have some significance to the plot, e.g.

What is the significance of this event/detail?
How does it connect with other details?
What is this preparing us for? What could happen?
What are we learning about this character?

Journals can also be used to record any favourite parts of a story. A page for 'Great Beginnings' or 'Favourite Descriptions' can provide a focus on the use of particular words or groups of words that have had an impact on the reader.

Descriptions
Choose the description you like the most in the story. In your journal write some words or phrases that helped to create a picture in your mind.

Picture clues
Look at one of the illustrations in the text. In your journal write all the things that the picture tells you that are not written in the text. Tell someone what you think the role of the illustrator is.

Character questions
Choose one character from the text and write some questions you would like to ask that character. Find two or three other people who have read the book and ask them the questions you have written. Were their answers what you expected?

Teachers often respond, in writing, to their students' journal entries and both teachers and students see this as a valuable activity.

Guiding Questions

The following activities are designed to help children in the planning stage of writing narratives.

Write some suggested questions on a chart and practise using them to help children talk through their story ideas with others.

Orientation

How will you start your story in a way that makes the reader want to read on?
What will your first sentence be?
When and where will your story begin?
What will the setting look like?
What words will you use to describe the setting and how can you help the reader paint a mind picture?

Characters

Who are the most important characters in the story?
What are they like?
What do they look like?
What sort of personalities do they have?
How do they talk in the story?

Complication

What problems does the main character need to overcome?

Story structure

What events happen first, next, last?
What does the main character do? Does he/she act and react in a believable way?
How will you describe the actions?

Resolution

How will things work out?
What loose ends will need to be tidied?
How will your story end?

Character Profiles

Model how to construct a character profile and encourage children to keep adding to their profiles.

Model the use of questions such as:
What do the characters look like?
How do they act?
How do they react?
What sort of personality traits are important to the story?
How do they get along with the other characters?
How do they think?

Encourage children to reflect on these questions as they read, to see how authors have constructed characters in the story.

Complications

Children sometimes have difficulty writing a complication and resolution in a story. The following activity follows the pattern of narrative and will enable children to practise building complications and resolving them. Choose issues from Health or Social Studies to provide meaningful topics for discussion.

Children work with a partner and design an argument by taking turns to add written dialogue. Only five turns each are allowed.

Turns 1–3   introduce characters and start actions that will lead to a conflict
Turns 4–6   increase tension to a climax
Turns 7–8   climax of argument
Turns 9–10   resolution of argument

Pass It On

The children sit in small groups They all write the first sentence of a story in which they set the scene and name two characters (one male and one female) e.g. *Once, long ago in a small country town Jessie and Tom were hiding in the shed near the farmhouse.*

Children then fold back the section on which they have written so that it can't be seen and pass their paper to the next person who writes a sentence beginning with 'suddenly'. *Suddenly a large brown snake slithered by.*

Repeat the procedure—folding, passing and adding sentences beginning 'She said', 'After that' and 'In the end'. Children then unfold the paper they have, and read the 'narrative' to the group.

Improving Narrative Writing

The following activities can be incorporated in modelled and shared writing sessions within the context of the classroom using children's own texts or with commercial texts introduced in shared reading sessions. They are suggestions that may be used for individual children, small groups or whole classes to cater for specific needs as they arise.

Sentence Manipulation

Time spent on sentence manipulation activities will help children understand sentence structure. Excerpts from texts used in shared reading sessions, newstelling or from children's own writing will provide authentic contexts for these activities. They are suitable for whole class small group and individual activities.

One way to make these activities easy to conduct is to use a sentence maker that can be made by using a holding strip to accommodate cards bearing words. The words need to be visible and easily moved.

Sentence expansion
Use the sentence maker to enhance the meaning of simple sentences by adding appropriate adjectives and adverbs.

Sentence completion
This activity focuses on the use of various conjunctions that signal what is to come. Conjunctions may signal cause and effect, time order sequence, additional or conditional information to follow.

Choose a sentence beginning from a story and then add various conjunctions. Children complete the sentence orally and discuss how and why the endings were different, e.g. The old haunted house was empty

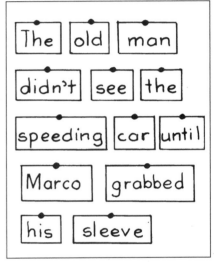

Sentence Maker (see also page 154)

but …
because …
and …
although …
while …
however …
so …
whether…
after…
therefore…

Sentence combining
This strategy is used to help children recognise the difference between 'talk written down' and written language structures. Johnson (1988, p. 22) states, 'The research consistently shows that having children combine simple sentences into complex ones has a beneficial effect on writing ability'.

From children's writing, take a sample that has a series of short sentences. Display using overhead projector or blackboard. Ask children to combine the ideas into one sentence. Begin with two or three sentences and then move to more. Model the strategy until children understand the technique. e.g.

Sam had a dog.
It was big.

Sam had a big dog.

Michael and David were worried.
Their pet snake had escaped from its cage.
It was probably somewhere in the house.
Mum would not be pleased if she found the snake in the potato bag.

Michael and David, whose pet snake had escaped from its cage and probably entered the house, were worried that their mother would find the creature in the potato bag.

Mr Brown was angry
His wife was flying home from Singapore.
The aircraft he had to meet was running late.
Mr Brown rang the airport for the latest information on the arrival time of the plane.
The information on arrival times was not up-to-date.

Mr Brown, who had rung the airport for information on the arrival time of his wife's flight from Singapore, was angry because the information given was not current.

Many different sentences can be made from the starting text. There is more than one correct sentence. Children should be encouraged to share and compare their sentences as discussion that follows will help them clarify understandings about written language.

Word Study

Many Early and Conventional writers need to extend their word knowledge so that they can elaborate their stories and make them more successful. Try the following activities.

Synonym substitution
Delete all of one particular part of speech from a text (adjectives or adverbs are good to start with) and ask children to list all the words they can think of that would make sense. Children then refer to the original text and compare their words with those used by the author. Discuss similarities and differences.

Antonym substitution
Children work in small groups using a familiar story and substitute opposites for each adjective or adverb in the story. They then read their version to another group and discuss the different versions.

Words instead of 'said'
Narrative writing ideally will to be linked to reading of narrative texts so children can start to note words that authors use instead of 'said'.

During shared reading sessions cover all the synonyms in the text that could be replaced with 'said'. Ask children to suggest words that would fit. Write the words as they are suggested and then check to see which one the author chose. Discuss why each word was used.

Descriptions that work
Have a scrap book available in the class library and encourage children to write any descriptive passages that they encounter in their reading. Encourage children to write the name of the book, page number and the author.

Descriptive language

Conventional and Proficient Phase writers may benefit from explicit demonstrations of sentence expansion activities that lead them to think about ways they can help readers paint images in their minds. They need to use their imagination and creativity to create a world where feelings, thoughts, words, actions, reactions are woven in such a way that the reader is compelled to read on. Good narrative texts do much more than list events; they somehow change the reader.

Past tense

Many narrative texts are written in the past tense so word sorts based on past tense verbs from a story will focus children's attention on common letter patterns such as the double consonant followed by the 'ed' inflectional ending. Phonetic spellers will benefit from these studies.

Using Direct Speech

Direct speech is used frequently in narratives and Early Phase writers often experiment with the use of direct speech so it is a good time to draw children's attention to various aspects of its use.

Reasons for using direct speech

Early Writers often overuse direct speech in their stories to the extent that their texts become difficult to follow. This is a quite natural part of their writing development and provides teachers with the opportunity to highlight passages of direct speech in published texts so they can elicit from children why the author has included that particular piece of dialogue. Children need to understand that authors usually include dialogue to enhance the plot by moving the story along or to tell the reader more about a character in the story.

Punctuation of direct speech

During shared reading draw children's attention to passages which contain direct speech. Ask children to work in small groups to try and work out what punctuation is used and where it is placed. Write all suggestions and ask children to formulate some rules or guidelines for punctuating direct speech. Check in other texts to see if rules seem to be legitimate and place rules in a class punctuation guidelines book for future reference.

One group of year six children devised this list:

Quotation marks come at the beginning and end of what each person says.

A new paragraph is started for each new speaker.

There's a comma before the speaking if it isn't the beginning of the sentence, e.g. Last night Mrs Parker yelled, 'Come here at once!'

If the talking goes on for more than a paragraph the quotation marks are put at the beginning of each paragraph but only at the end of the last one.

These observations provided a starting point for further studies and because the children had discovered the rules they were quite excited about using, reviewing and adding to them.

The problem-solving approach can be adapted and used to teach the function of other punctuation marks.

Planning Frameworks

Encourage children to use planning frameworks (see pages 37–9) to make a story outline or to draw events in the story.

How the Galah Became Bink and Gray

Long ago in the land of Wonga there lived an artist who had many different colours. His paints didn't come off things. All the birds, including the white galah, watched the artist paint. He painted the butterflies wings and he painted sculptures of paddocks and meadows. One day while flying around the white galah was wondering how he could get some pretty colours like the butterfly. The white galah went to ask the king and queen fairy of the forest if he could get permission off the artist to paint him yellow and purple. They said no because they thought that the animals and birds should stay the colour they are there. The poor white galah went back home and was sad, so he went to bed. He got out of bed and went outside. An eagle tried to get him by swooping down and clawing the galah. The galah just kept running forwards instead of going back to his house. He accidentally ran into the gray and pink paint the artist had left outside It tipped all over the white galah and the galah became pink and gray. The artist was angry because the galah had ruined his beautiful paint, but the galah was happy because he wasn't white any longer. That's how we see the galah today with its beatiful pink and gray feathers

A lovely tale – well told too!
Well done!

NARRATIVE PLAN

FRAMEWORK HEADINGS	MAKE NOTES OR DRAWINGS TO HELP PLAN YOUR STORY
Title	
Orientation	
Initiating Event	
Complication	
Resolution	
Coda/Moral/Concluding statement	

NARRATIVE PLAN

NAME: **DATE:**

TITLE:

ORIENTATION:

Setting: Who? When? Where? What? Why?

_____

_____

_____

_____

_____

_____

_____

_____

_____

_____

INITIATING EVENT

What began the event? How did the characters get involved?

_____

_____

_____

_____

_____

_____

_____

_____

_____

COMPLICATION/S:
How the conflict/s or problem/s began

_____

_____

_____

_____

_____

_____

_____

_____

_____

RESOLUTION:
How the character/s solve the conflict/s or problem/s.

_____

_____

_____

_____

_____

_____

_____

_____

_____

_____

_____

_____

Assessment and Evaluation of Narrative Writing

The continuum of indicators on the following page traces the development of Narrative writing. Teachers may wish to use the indicators to assess children's control of Narrative writing.

Samples of the combined use of the *Writing: Developmental Continuum* and the continuum for Narrative writing are included on pages 42–3 to show how teachers use a combination of both to evaluate children's writing. It is suggested that samples of work be examined and indicators highlighted. This information provides a basis for teaching and enables teachers to help children see how their writing can be improved.

A checklist for Narratives is provided on page 44. This is made up of the indicators for the Extending stage of Narrative writing and can be used as a quick way of assessing children's progress in the writing of Narrative texts.

NARRATIVE INDICATORS

BEGINNING

Purpose:

The writer:
- discusses why stories are written

Text Organisation and Content
- writes a series of loosely connected events or actions concluding with a simple ending

Orientation
- includes partial information about story context expecting that the reader shares background
- finds it difficult to describe characters as separate beings with emotions

Complication
- writes a sequence of events that do not seem to be leading to a complication
- focuses on one or two characters with no elaboration or description
- includes characters that only perform actions but generally gives no details of reactions
- has difficulty expressing information that is generally conveyed in face-to-face conversations, e.g. absence of punctuation and adjectives to communicate things like gesture and facial expression

Resolution
- writes a simple ending, e.g. 'I woke up.'
- finds it difficult to write an ending

Language Features
- uses a few basic connectives e.g. *and, then*
- changes from writing in third person to writing in the first person
- rarely uses direct speech
- has some difficulty in maintaining consistent tense

DEVELOPING

Purpose:

The writer:
- discusses why stories are written

Text Organisation and Content
- introduces the characters and settings and focuses on a series of actions that lead to a complication and simple resolution

Orientation
- writes a title
- attempts to orient the reader with some details of setting
- includes essentials of time, place and characters with little elaboration or description
- writes about stereotypes, e.g. the wicked witch, the brave prince, etc.

Complication
- includes initiating event leading to limited development of complication
- includes particular features of well-known narrative forms, e.g. fairy stories—rhyme, rhythm and repetition—'Run, run as fast as you can . . .'
- copies complications from well-known stories
- relies almost entirely on actions of the characters to develop plot
- introduces characters without indicating where they came from or why they have appeared

Resolution
- attempts resolution of story; ending is often predictable and not very successful, e.g. 'It was a dream.'
- uses recurring themes, e.g. good triumphs over evil

Language Features
- uses a limited number of adjectives and adverbs to provide some description
- writes conversation but the reader has difficulty in deciding who said what
- attempts direct speech, exclamation and question marks to enhance meaning and create atmosphere
- uses causal conjunctions e.g. *so, because, if . . . .*

CONSOLIDATING

Purpose:

The writer:
- demonstrates understanding that stories may be written to entertain, teach, inform, reflect on, experience and to activate or extend the reader's imagination

Text Organisation and Content
- orients the reader by the inclusion of details selected to enhance development of the story. Complications are introduced and resolved in a satisfying way

Orientation
- writes a suitable title
- includes details of time, place and characters with elaboration to establish the context for reader
- includes details of setting that affect the development of the plot
- uses descriptive detailed characterisation
- assumes understanding of character stereotypes, e.g. 'Witches are mean.'

Complication
- includes initiating event developed into a complication
- extends the plot by including more than one complication

Resolution
- withholds some information to build or maintain tension
- makes use of environmental factors to build suspense, e.g. 'thunder rolled, lightning flashed . . .'
- attempts to tie elements together to draw the story towards a conclusion
- may include evaluative comments or coda (reflective statement)
- shows interplay between characters and conflicts and resolves at least some of the conflicts

Language Features
- uses similes, adjectival and adverbial clauses and phrases to elaborate
- uses more complex conjunctions, e.g. *nevertheless . . ., otherwise*
- varies sentence length and punctuation to change tempo

EXTENDING

Purpose:

The writer:
- demonstrates understanding that stories may be written for many purposes and that readers interpret stories in different ways

Text Organisation and Content
- chooses to use, manipulate or abandon conventional text organisation to achieve impact

Orientation
- uses title to tantalise the reader; title may have a dual meaning, e.g. The Last Race
- shows evidence of innovative use of story elements
- provides appropriate detail to establish relationships between setting, and major and minor characters
- generalises on attitude or disposition

Complication
- develops a story line that is cohesive and coherent and elaborates and resolves each complication in episodes
- invites reader to fill in details
- manipulates the audience by the use of suspense, selectively disclosing information
- develops characters and gives them substance according to their importance to the theme or plot
- provides insight into characters' feelings

Resolution
- ties elements together to draw the story towards a conclusion
- shows interplay between characters and conflicts and resolves conflicts
- is able to interpret events imaginatively

Language Features
- effectively controls language and structural features and elicits emotional responses from readers by careful selection of vocabulary and writing style
- draws the reader into the narrative by the use of various devices such as imagery, metaphor and simile
- makes effective use of dialogue and characters with elaboration to establish the context for reader

Sample of Narrative writing:

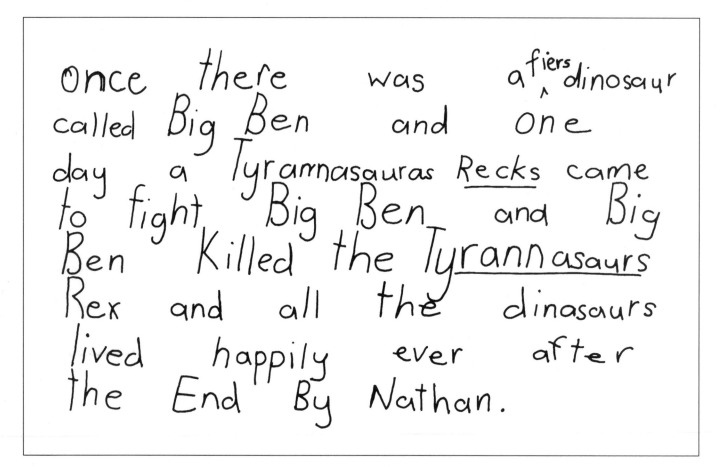

Once there was a fiers dinosaur called Big Ben and one day a Tyrannasauras Recks came to fight Big Ben and Big Ben Killed the Tyrannasaurs Rex and all the dinasaurs lived happily ever after the End By Nathan.

Early Writing Phase Indicators from Writing: Developmental Continuum highlighted:

The writer:
- ◆ **uses a small range of familiar text forms**
- ◆ **chooses topics that are personally significant**
- • uses a partial organisational framework, e.g. simple orientation and story development
- • is beginning to use some narrative structure
- ◆ **experiments with words drawn from language experience activities, literature, media and oral language of peers and others**
- ◆ **begins to develop editing skills**
- ◆ **attempts to use some punctuation**

Narrative Continuum Indicators (Beginning) highlighted:

The writer:
- • discusses why stories are written
- • writes a series of loosely connected events or actions concluding with a simple ending
- • includes partial information about story context expecting that the reader shares background
- • focuses on one or two characters with no elaboration or description
- • includes characters that only perform actions but generally gives no details of reactions
- • has difficulty expressing information that is generally conveyed in face-to-face conversations, e.g. absence of punctuation and adjective to communicate things like gesture and facial expression
- • writes a simple ending, e.g. 'I woke up'
- • uses a few basic connectives e.g. *and*, *then*

This page provides an example of the combined use of the *Writing: Developmental Continuum* and the continuum for Narrative writing, to evaluate children's writing. It confirms placement on *Writing: Developmental Continuum* and can be used to assess control of Narrative writing.

Sample of Narrative writing:

Passive Emotions
A story to promote non-smoking

The small lounge-room was completely dark except for a thin strip of dismal, grey light which shone through a gap between the curtains from a street lamp outside. The room was shrouded in smoke, cigarette smoke. It was thickest in the darkest corner of the room. In this corner, sitting in a rocking chair, was a balding, middle-aged man.

The few thin strands of his hair lifted in the slight breeze created by a fan standing across the room. His clothes reeked of the foul smelling smoke. His wrinkled face looked as if he was mourning something, or someone, he had cherished. He seemed oblivious to the world around him, lost deep in his mind and memories of a happier past.

A tear trickled slowly down his cheek while his eyes were locked on a photograph he was holding in his hand. From the picture a beautiful young bride in a floral dress smiled up at him. She had been his wife and he had loved her like life itself. Two days ago she had died prematurely, and painfully, from lung cancer.

'Smoking related' the doctor had said. Yet she had never once smoked in all her life. She had been a passive smoker.

He remembered how they used to sit together, arms around each other. As he enjoyed his cigarettes she would inhale the smoke he expelled. Throughout their twenty years of happy marriage she had continually, gently, lovingly urged him to stop smoking, but all in vain. He had shunned the idea, never listening to her. She had always said smoking was endangering his life. Neither of them had imagined her life was under threat. Now she was gone from him forever.

He looked down at the cigarette in his hand and watched the white paper blackening and disappearing in smoke. The tiny red glow slowly burned its way towards his fingers, releasing the poisons which had killed her and were probably killing him. He felt the rage and grief well up inside him and focus on the tiny tube of tobacco. Then suddenly, with a violent jab of his hand, he crushed the murderous thing, extinguishing the burning tip, and cursed the day he had first set one of those deadly cigarettes to his lips.

Proficient Writing Phase Indicators from Writing: Developmental Continuum highlighted

The writer:

◆ **selects text forms to suit purpose and audience, demonstrating control over most essential elements**
- identifies likely audiences and adjusts writing to achieve impact
- conveys a sense of personal involvement in imaginative writing
- conducts research effectively in order to select appropriate information to fulfil task demands
◆ **writes to define, clarify and develop ideas and express creativity, e.g. stories, poems, reports, arguments**
- has sufficient quality ideas to fulfil task demands
- develops topic fully
- sustains coherence and cohesion throughout text
◆ **writes a topic sentence and includes relevant information to develop a cohesive paragraph**
◆ **organises paragraphs logically to form a cohesive text**
◆ **uses a variety of simple, compound and complex sentences appropriate to text form**
◆ **uses a wide range of words that clearly and precisely convey meaning in a particular form**
- sustains appropriate language throughout
◆ **edits own writing during and after composing**
◆ **demonstrates accurate use of punctuation**
◆ **takes notes, selects and synthesises relevant information and plans text sequence**

Narrative Continuum Indicators (Extending) highlighted:

The writer

- demonstrates understanding that stories may be written for many purposes and that readers interpret stories in different ways
- chooses to use, manipulate or abandon conventional text organisation to achieve impact
- uses title to tantalise the reader; title may have a dual meaning, e.g. The Last Race
- shows evidence of innovative use of story elements
- provides appropriate detail to establish relationships between setting, and major and minor characters
- generalises on attitude or disposition
- develops a story line that is cohesive and coherent and elaborates and resolves each complication in episodes
- invites reader to fill in details
- manipulates the audience by the use of suspense, selectively disclosing information
- provides insight into characters' feelings
- ties elements together to draw the story towards a conclusion
- is able to interpret events imaginatively
- effectively controls language and structural features
- elicits emotional responses from readers by careful selection of vocabulary and writing style
- draws the reader into the narrative by the use of various devices such as imagery, metaphor and simile

This page provides an example of the combined use of the *Writing: Developmental Continuum* and the continuum for Narrative writing, to evaluate a sample of writing. It confirms placement on the *Writing: Developmental Continuum* and can be used to assess control of Narrative writing.

CHECKLIST FOR NARRATIVES	ALWAYS	SOMETIMES	NOT YET

Purpose

The writer
- demonstrates understanding that stories may be written for many purposes and that readers interpret stories in different ways

Text Organisation and Content
- chooses to use, manipulate or abandon conventional text organisation to achieve impact

Orientation
- uses title to tantalise the reader; title may have a dual meaning, e.g. The Last Race
- shows evidence of innovative use of story elements
- provides appropriate detail to establish relationships between setting, and major and minor characters
- generalises on attitude or disposition

Complication
- develops a story line that is cohesive and coherent and elaborates and resolves each complication in episodes
- invites reader to fill in details
- manipulates the audience by the use of suspense, selectively disclosing information
- develops characters and gives them substance according to their importance to the theme or plot
- provides insight into characters' feelings

Resolution
- ties elements together to draw the story towards a conclusion
- shows interplay between characters and conflicts and resolves conflicts
- is able to interpret events imaginatively

Language Features
- effectively controls language and structural features and elicits emotional responses from readers by careful selection of vocabulary and writing style
- draws the reader into the narrative by the use of various devices such as imagery, metaphor and simile
- makes effective use of dialogue and characters with elaboration to establish the context for reader

 © Education Department of Western Australia. Published by Rigby Heinemann

Chapter 4:

Recounts

A recount is the retelling or recounting of past experiences. Recounts are generally based on the direct experiences of the author but may also be imaginative or outside the author's experience. Young children often write recounts which follow directly from their 'newstelling'.

Features of a Recount

Purpose
The purpose of a recount is to tell what happened and this may involve the author's personal interpretation of events.

Focus
Sequential specific events

Types
There are different types of recounts:

Personal recounts recounting an experience in which the author has been directly involved

Factual recounts retelling an event or incident such as a newspaper report, an accident report

Imaginative recounts taking on a fictitious role and relating imaginary events, e.g. a day in the life of a new puppy

Examples
Recounts may be in the form of biographies, autobiographies, newspaper reports of events, histories, letters, diaries, journals, eye-witness accounts of incidents, accounts of accidents submitted for insurance claims.

Text Organisation
Recounts generally begin with a **Setting** or **Orientation** that includes background information to assist the reader's understanding of the recount. There are usually details about Who? When? Where? Why?

Important **Events** are then elaborated and usually arranged in chronological order, first to last. The events are presented in an interesting way and may include personal comments.

Many recounts have an **Evaluative Comment** or **Concluding Statement** that may simply be a comment on the preceding set of events but this is optional. It is often a comment that reflects the author's feelings about the preceding events described.

Language Features

- Includes specific participants (my family)
- Usually written in simple past tense
- Use of dynamic or action verbs, e.g. *went, saw, fed, returned*
- Use of linking words to do with time provides the cohesive ties in the text, e.g. *yesterday, when, after, before, during*
- Use of first person personal pronouns I/we
- Details are selected to add interest
- Personal responses to the event may be included (except in factual recounts)

(Adapted from Derewianka B. 1990 *Exploring How Texts Work*, pages 15 and 16.)

RECOUNT

A trip to the zoo.

Yesterday my family went to the zoo to see the elephant.

When we got to the zoo, we went to the shop to buy some food to give to the animals.

After getting the food we went to the nocturnal house where we saw some birds and reptiles which only come out at night.

Before lunch we went for a ride on the elephant. It was a thrill to ride it. Dad nearly fell off when he let go of the rope.

During lunch we fed some birds in the park.

In the afternoon we saw the animals being fed.

When we returned home we were very tired but happy because we had so much fun.

RECOUNT

- **Setting**
  - Who?
  - Where?
  - When?
  - Why?
- **Events in Time Order**
  (i.e., First to Last)
  1.,
  2.,
  3.,...etc.
- **Concluding Statement/Ending**

Recount Framework

Title: summarises the text

A Trip to the Zoo

Setting tells:
when? who?
where? why?

Text cohesion is provided by linking words of time

<u>Yesterday</u> my family went to the zoo to see the elephant.

<u>When</u> we got to the zoo, we went to the shop to buy some food to give to the animals. ← Event

<u>After</u> getting the food we went to the nocturnal house where we saw some birds and reptiles which only come out at night. ← Event

Written in the past tense

Before lunch we went for a fide on the elephant. It was great fun. Dad nearly fell off when he let go of the rope. ← Event

Paragraphs in time order sequence

<u>During</u> lunch we fed some birds in the park. In the afternoon we saw some animals being fed. ← Event

<u>When</u> we returned home we were very tired but happy because we had so much fun. ← Conclusion

Action words: saw, fed, returned

Framework and text written by Dr Peter Sloan and Dr Ross Latham for the First Steps Project.

A Trip to the Zoo

Yesterday my family went to the zoo to see the elephant.

When we got to the zoo, we went to the shop to buy some food to give to the animals.

After getting the food we went to the nocturnal house where we saw some birds and reptiles which only come out at night.

Before lunch we went for a ride on the elephant. It was a thrill to ride it. Dad nearly fell off when he let go of the rope.

During lunch we fed some birds in the park.

In the afternoon we saw the animals being fed.

When we returned home we were very tired but happy because we had so much fun.

This simple text uses a recognisable Recount framework and may be used by teachers to introduce and analyse the features of a Recount. See activities on page 54.

Written by Dr Peter Sloan and Dr Ross Latham for the First Steps Project.

Exploring and Planning Recounts

Recounts are one of the most common language forms used by children. When children at home recall events in which they have participated they are recounting experiences. In the classroom newstelling provides an ideal context for exposing children to the oral recounts which lead easily into the written form.

Activities

Teachers may choose a number of different ways of helping children explore recounts. Several suggestions are included in this section. Teachers will, of course, adapt any suggestions to suit their particular children's needs. The activities can be used for small groups of children, for individuals or for whole classes.

Role Play and Experimental Phase writers can begin to prepare for written recounts by 'telling news' at home and in the classroom.

Oral news

Early Phase writers will benefit from the following activities.

News plan

Wall diaries

Draw and tell

Teachers may help Early, Conventional and Proficient writers to improve their recount writing by the use of some of the following approaches.

Direct model

Text reconstruction

Directed reading

Modelled writing

Notebooks

Wall diaries

Draw and rell

Oral News

For children in Role Play and Experimental Phases of writing, teacher modelling of what to include in oral newstelling will help to develop understanding of the structure of recounts.

A newstelling chart that includes *who*, *when*, *where*, *why* and *what* will help children focus on the necessary content to include in their retelling.

To introduce the chart, explain why it is necessary to include background information for the audience (orientation).

Model how to tell news and explain the links between the information supplied and key words included on the chart. Include *when*, *who*, *where*, *what* and *why* in the news and point to each area of the chart as appropriate.

Repeat the procedure a number of times and be explicit about the structure of the news.

Choose children to tell news and ask the audience to identify which elements have been included and to ask questions about any that have been omitted.

Things to look for
The children:

- introduce a topic appropriately
- produce appropriately sequenced recounts
- use vocabulary related to time, e.g. *first, next, then*
- monitor news as a listener and formulate appropriate questions
- understand special terminology used at newstime, e.g. *when, why, feelings*

Framework for Planning News Content

Generating Writing from a News Plan

The same news framework can be used by Early Phase writers to plan their written recounts. The use of a planning framework will help these writers to select relevant details to be included in their recount.

Model the use of the framework by jotting key words or drawing pictures to represent key information.

Use the plan to write the news in full to demonstrate the transition of a plan to a written text.

Encourage children to use the plan when they write their own recounts of excursions, diary entries, recounts of their day (The plan is meant only to be used until children feel confident about details they need to include).

When children have completed their draft writing ask them to use the plan to check that all details are included.

When	Where	What	Who with	Why
Last Tuesday	on the driveway		no one	have fun going fast
After School	it is gery	Skatbrooding	just me	
/ Ring / Ring	it is long	Pink Windy		
I ran home				

My news plan.

Last Tuesday I ran home when the siren rang at school. At home I was playing on my skateboard on the driveway outside my house. My driveway is grey and it is long and the skateboard is pink The weather was windy. No one was with me, and I had fun because I was going fast.

Examples of teacher modelling

Explaining the purpose of the plan

> Teacher: *I'm not going to say my news immediately. I'm going to get my news ready first. I'm going to think about all the things I want to say and draw some pictures to help me remember them.*

Modelling how to start a news plan

> Teacher: *I'm going to think of some interesting words to use to describe how I felt when...*
> *I'm going to see if I can remember some more things to talk about for what I did.*

Explaining how to complete a news plan

> Teacher: *I'm not going to write the whole sentence on my plan. I'm just going to put some words to remind me what to say.*

Explaining how to use a plan when presenting

> Teacher: *Have a quick look at your plan before you tell us your news. Are you ready? Put your plan down on the table.*

My News Plan				
When?	**Who?**	**Where?**	**What?**	**Why?**

Planning for News: Year 1

NEWS PLAN FOR A RECOUNT

MY NEWS PLAN				
When?	**Who?**	**Where?**	**What?**	**Why?**

53

The sample text A Trip to the Zoo (on page 48) may be used for the following introductory activities.

Direct Model

Present an example of a complete, accurate and easily distinguished recount. Discuss the text in detail and have children discover the kind of information in each paragraph.

Read each paragraph and ask:
What does it tell you?
What is its purpose?

Attach framework labels to each paragraph, e.g. Setting, Event 1, Event 2...

Talk about the linking words to do with time.

Talk about texts written in the past tense.

Text Reconstruction

Children work in small groups to reconstruct a text from jumbled paragraphs.

Discuss clues they used to order the text. (Linking words of time.)

Examine the first and last sentences in each paragraph to show the links.

Reading

Select recounts and use a directed silent reading approach or shared reading to ask questions based on recount framework headings.

Also ask questions such as:
Why did the author include this part?
How would the author have decided what details to include?
How did the author decide on that title?
Can you think of another title?
What other questions would you have asked the author?

Ask children to hunt for 'time words' list and sort them to construct a word bank for later use. Encourage children to add to the word bank.

Modelled Writing

Choose events in which the children are interested and model the writing of recounts. Model personal recounts, factual recounts and imaginary recounts.

Mention such items as the title, the contents of each paragraph, the selection of relevant details to include, the use of a variety of linking words to do with time, how to get rid of 'and then' and ways to order the information.

Notebooks

Encourage children to carry a small notebook and jot down anything that they may be able to use in their writing.

Wall Diaries

Start a class wall diary and add entries each day. At the end of the week staple pages together and place the 'Class News' in the book corner.

Draw and Tell

In groups of four ask children to draw their news (using headings from the recount framework) and then give their drawings to a partner who has to tell the news to the rest of the group using only the drawings. Use planning sheets to focus attention on relevant details.

Exploring Recounts—a sample unit

This sample unit includes ideas for writing, reading, speaking and listening. It is assumed that teachers will adapt sessions to suit the needs of the children in their class.

The objective in these sessions was to introduce children to one way of presenting information they had gathered. When students have been exposed to a number of alternative forms they should be encouraged to choose the form that best suits the audience and purpose of the writing.

In this instance the teacher was preparing her students for an excursion to a nearby ice cream factory. The students were from a wide variety of ethnic backgrounds and many of the children didn't speak English at home. They had previously used the newstelling chart to help them with oral news and enjoyed writing especially when they could share their work with others. Most of their writing in previous years had been 'free choice' writing and some children had difficulty with the organisation of writing and the selection of relevant details to include. The students were keen to contribute their class news (recounts) to the school paper that was to be published at the end of term so the teacher decided to concentrate on recounts.

During the time before the excursion the teacher read recounts from the newspaper and discussed the contents relating them to the already familiar newstelling chart. In modelled writing sessions the teacher wrote personal recounts and these were left on display. After maths time children were asked to write in their journal 'What I did today in maths' and for health they kept a diary of food and exercise for one day. For serial reading the teacher read *Penny Pollard's Diary*.

A trip to an ice cream factory was planned as part of a Social Studies unit. Children in the class had been involved in the preparations for the trip. They had written letters to invite parent helpers, organised the bus, worked out costs, sought permission to travel and attended to other details of the excursion. To introduce written recounts the teacher planned the following sequence of language activities.

Objective: to establish the purpose and audience for writing and to explore the features of a recount using a problem-solving approach.
Discussion was initiated about how the class could tell others in the school about their trip. The children decided to write articles for the weekly newsletter and the school paper. The teacher introduced the word 'recount' and mentioned that she had some recounts from another class who had visited the same factory previously.

The children were keen to see what other children had done. Each child was given a copy of four recounts (samples 1–4 on page 56). They then used a problem solving approach to analyse them. At the end of the session they had produced a draft chart of 'Rules for Recounts.'

SAMPLE 1

A Good Day

We went to an ice cream factory and I got a free hat and an ice cream.

The video was good.

The factory was good.

The bus ride was boring.

The day was good.

I wanted to go in the freezer but I couldn't go in because I wasn't allowed. I picked a drumstick and the cone was crunchy.

SAMPLE 2

A Visit

We went to an ice cream factory. We caught the bus and the driver was making jokes. Some kids were a bit noisy so the teacher told them off. The bus ride was good. It started to rain just when we got near the place but it stopped when we were getting out.

The first thing was getting a free hat then watching a video. After that we walked around the factory and some kids were aloud to taste some new ice cream. Moroni, Elspeth and Jenny tasted it. The machines were big and some ladies were putting stuff in boxes and they had hats on so their hair couldn't get in anything. I got a free ice cream and then we went home.

SAMPLE 3

A Trip to the Ice Cream Factory

Yesterday our class went to Peters ice cream factory in Balcatta.

First we got on the bus then we started off. We got to the factory and went in. Then we were given a hat and then we watched a video about making ice creams.

Our class was split into two groups and then we were shown around the factory. Then we saw some old photos from the olden days. We looked through a big window. They were making roll ice creams for the Japanese market. Then we saw all different machines and how the ice creams were wrapped and packed. Then we went to the cafeteria and got a free ice cream.

SAMPLE 4

Our Visit to an Ice Cream Factory

Yesterday the children from Room 10 went by bus to Peters ice cream factory in Balcatta to find out how ice cream was made.

When we arrived we all got a free hat and then watched a video about making ice cream. The lady showed us some new products and some people were allowed to taste them I didn't like the Green Tea ice cream at all!

After the video session we split into two groups and a lady showed us around the factory and explained how ice cream was made. It was quite interesting to look through the windows but we couldn't get near the ice creams. I found out that Peters export a lot of ice cream to Asian and other countries.

Before we left we went to the cafeteria and were allowed to choose a free ice cream. We all sat on the lawn and ate it. My ice cream was a chocolate drumstick it was delicious.

As soon as everyone had finished eating we got on the bus and went back to school.

Children read the four recounts and after discussions with other members of the group they ranked the recounts from least effective to most effective. They discussed the one which they felt was least effective first.

Sample 1
The children said:
Number 1 was the worst because the title
wasn't any help and it didn't say who went
to the factory or when they went.

The teacher wrote:
Title doesn't tell enough.
Not enough information given about the setting.

It didn't really tell you what happened
Things were out of order.

Events were not mentioned in order.

It shouldn't have the bit about wanting
to go in the freezer.

Some irrelevant details were included.

The children then worked through the other samples discussing the comparative merits of each. They decided that **Sample 4** was the best and gave their reasons

Children said:
Number 4 is the best because the title helps us
to know what the recount is about and
important information about who, when,
where, what and why are in the first sentence.

Teacher wrote:
Title summarises the text.
Setting includes information that tells
who, when, where, what and why.

It tells all the things they did.

Events are described in time order.

Each bit tells us about a different part of the trip.

Each paragraph is on a different part of the topic. At the end of the session the children had produced a chart which they called 'Our Rules for Writing Recounts'.

Over time a collection of charts for other forms of writing can be accumulated and children will refer to the writing charts as 'Our charts—the ones we made up' and take great pride in telling any interested visitor that they make the charts in their room. The charts are used often because children have ownership of them and see them as greatly assisting their writing.

Children were asked where they might find recounts being used. They suggested newspapers, journals and diaries might contain recounts. The teacher asked them to start collecting any recounts they saw.

Objective: to plan a recount

After returning from the excursion the students and teacher talked about the important things they wished to mention in their recounts. Suggestions were written as key words and placed in time order for children's reference. The teacher modelled writing a recount using ideas from the planning sheet.

Objective: to find a range of words instead of 'then'

In oral newstelling (and in personal writing) many students overused the word 'then' so the teacher used modelled and shared writing of a recount to focus on this problem. Children were invited to make suggestions for improving the recount. Children worked in small groups to brainstorm words instead of 'then' All words were displayed. Children were able to enter any words they thought they might use into their Spelling Journals.

Objective: to find common letter patterns in past tense verbs—Word Study

Teacher referred to modelled recount from previous day and asked students to look for the verbs. These were circled and then copied by the teacher. As they were past tense verbs many of them ended with 'ed'. The Phonetic spellers having difficulty with the 'ed' inflectional endings then worked with the teacher using those words as a basis for word sorts and focusing on the common letter patterns, e.g. sto*pped*, sli*pped*, fini*shed*, wat*ched*, hu*rried*, while the rest of the class looked for recounts in newspapers. During sharing time the Phonetic spellers were able to talk about their discoveries and the whole class was invited to make a rule about some words that ended in 'ed'. Children then tested their rules by reading books and modified their rules.

Objective: to improve children's writing by analysing and manipulating sentences (small groups of children chosen on basis of need)

Sentence manipulation

Time spent on sentence manipulation activities will help children understand sentence structure. Excerpts from texts used in shared reading sessions, newstelling or from children's own writing will provide authentic contexts for these activities. They are suitable for whole class, small group and individual activities.

One way to make these activities easy to conduct is to use a sentence maker that can be made by using a holding strip to accommodate cards bearing words (see page 33). The words need to be visible and easily moved.

Sentence transformation
Singular to plural
Some children (particularly Early Writers) need to see what happens when the subject of the sentence changes from singular to plural. The sentence maker can be used to demonstrate these changes e.g.
She was going.
We were going.

Tenses
Maintenance of consistent tense throughout a story may be difficult for some children so sentence makers can be used to demonstrate the construction in the three main tenses, e.g.
I am going to the zoo.
I went to the zoo.
I shall go to the zoo.

If these are left in an accessible place children can continue to manipulate the cards to make new sentences

Objective: to write a recount of class visit
Independent writing
Children used recount planning sheets for drawings or key words to remind them of the main events they wished to include. They shared their plans and helped each other to remember the important parts

Children then began to write their draft. During this time the teacher was able to hold conferences and attend to individual needs of children who required specific help.

Objective: to revise and edit recounts
Revision and evaluation
Some children were ready to revise and edit their draft writing so the teacher modelled some editing techniques using the modelled text from the first day. Children were encouraged to use the editing checklist they had devised previously. They resumed their writing and those who were ready revised their writing by consulting the 'Rules for Writing Recounts' chart and 'Editing Checklist' and made any necessary adjustments.

Objective: to analyse other contexts in which recounts are used
Children read and shared recounts they had found in newspapers, books and diaries. They took great delight in finding whether the orientation included all important details and then looked to see if the events were in chronological order. They also made judgements about headlines, titles and concluding paragraphs. They added any new ' time words' to their list of 'words instead of *then* chart'.

In shared reading time some children cut up newspaper articles they had collected and gave them to others to reconstruct. This activity generated discussion about the construction of recounts. Students discussed why they had assembled the recounts in a particular way and noted the linking words that assisted them. They also discovered how one paragraph linked to the next.

Elective Activities

Objective: to allow students time to further explore features of recounts
Children were free to complete their recount, learn to spell any words with which they were having difficulties and to follow their own investigations. Some students also decided to start looking for alternatives for overused words in their writing. Words they targeted were 'nice', 'fun', 'happy'. They started a Class Thesaurus with lists of alternatives and shared these with others in the class. Some children managed to find (and read) a number of books that were personal, imaginative or factual recounts. Others decided to begin an imaginative recount which they decided should be called 'The Day That Room 10 Came to My Factory' written by I. Scream. Another group decided to keep collecting past tense verbs and categorising them according to their spelling. Some children went through newspapers with highlighter pens and found still more 'time' words which they added to the chart. When it was time for sharing they moved into small groups with representatives from each activity and presented what they had been doing to others in the group.

Objective: to present information to an audience
Reading
Children visited various classes in the school and read their recounts. Some were chosen for the school newspaper and others displayed for parents at assembly.

Objective: to reflect on own knowledge and understandings
Reflection
Children were asked to write in their journals 'What I know about writing and reading recounts'. They then moved into groups of three and shared their journal entries. The teacher collected the journals and responded.

Planning Frameworks

Encourage children to use planning frameworks (see pages 61–2) to write or illustrate a recount outline.

RECOUNT PLAN

TOPIC:

1. SETTING: WHO? WHERE? WHEN? WHAT? WHY?

2. EVENTS IN TIME ORDER

Event 1

Event 2

Event 3

Event 4

3. CONCLUDING STATEMENT/ENDING

RECOUNT PLAN

Name: _____

ILLUSTRATION	OPENING STATEMENT (WHO? WHEN? WHERE? WHAT?)
	_____
	_____
	_____
	_____
ILLUSTRATION	**EVENT 1**
	_____
	_____
	_____
	_____
ILLUSTRATION	**EVENT 2**
	_____
	_____
	_____
	_____
ILLUSTRATION	**ENDING**
	_____
	_____
	_____
	_____

Assessment and Evaluation of Recount Writing

The continuum of indicators on the following page traces the development of Recount writing.

Samples of the combined use of the *Writing: Developmental Continuum* and the continuum for Recount writing are included on pages 65–6 to show how teachers use a combination of both to evaluate children's writing. It is suggested that samples of work be examined and indicators highlighted. This information provides a basis for teaching and enables teachers to help children see how their writing can be improved.

A checklist for Recounts is provided on page 67. This is made up of the indicators for the Extending stage of Recount writing and can be used as a quick way of assessing children's progress in writing Recount texts.

R E C O U N T   I N D I C A T O R S

BEGINNING

Purpose:
The writer:
- uses recounts to tell of a past experience

Text Organisation and Content
- writes a simple account with little description

Orientation
- provides little information about setting or the context in which the events happened, e.g. tells who and where but not when.

Events
- uses oral language structures, gives all events equal attention and importance, e.g. Dawn-to-dark accounts—'I got up. I went to the zoo. I came home.'
- links events chronologically

Evaluation (optional)
- writes an evaluative comment as a conclusion

Language Features
- uses oral language structures
- usually writes in the past tense
- uses little variety of linking words, e.g. *and, then*

DEVELOPING

Purpose:
The writer:
- uses recounts to reconstruct past events

Text Organisation and Content
- establishes time, place and participants of recount and includes events in sequence

Events
- writes additional information about more important events, e.g. 'My dad took me to the zoo. I saw all the animals. The elephant was the biggest and best animal. I liked the monkeys too. When it was dark, we went home.'
- includes only characters of significance to the recount

Evaluation (optional)
- writes a satisfactory conclusion

Language Features
- begins to use structures of written language
- uses some adverbs and adjectives to clarify meaning
- maintains tense
- uses action verbs and generally shows agreement between subject and verb, e.g. *I went, I saw, I did*
- uses a limited number of linking words, e.g. *and so, later, soon*
- writes complete sentences
- uses a variety of sentence lengths

CONSOLIDATING

Purpose:
The writer:
- demonstrates understanding that recounts can retell a personal experience, record particulars of an event, e.g. a football match, be an imaginative description of events
- demonstrates understanding that diaries, news reports, biographies, journals, may be recounts

Text Organisation and Content
- provides an orientation that is complete and succinct and includes significant events in chronological sequence

Orientation
- caters for reader by providing contextual details
- provides details of the environment that impact on the way events unfold

Events
- attempts to interpret events imaginatively, elaborating important events
- elaborates aspects of characters that affect events
- gives characters credibility by use of dialogue or significant actions, e.g. Mum said angrily, 'Come here at once!'
- sustains topic throughout

Evaluation (optional)
- writes more complex concluding statements with evaluative comment or summary

Language Features
- uses a variety of appropriate adjectival and adverbial phrases
- maintains consistent past tense
- uses a variety of action and process verbs, e.g. *I travelled, I glimpsed, I thought*
- varies conjunctions and linking words to indicate time, e.g. *soon, later, eventually*
- writes complete sentences that are increasingly complex
- groups sentences containing related information into paragraphs

EXTENDING

Purpose:
The writer:
- demonstrates understanding that recounts can be written for a number of purposes and audiences and that a writer's experiences influence what he/she writes

Text Organisation and Content
- organises the schematic structure of the recount by starting with an orientation that aims to interest the reader and including important events relating to a particular occasion

Orientation
- includes all relevant background information needed to understand the text, i.e. who was involved, when and where it happened and other pertinent details

Events
- develops the topic fully by including significant events chosen to add interest and impact
- elaborates events so that the reader is able to visualise the experience
- interprets events imaginatively, symbolically or metaphorically
- orders the events chronologically into easily followed sequential steps
- sometimes includes personal reflections or comments about events in the recount, e.g. it was a great honour....

Evaluation (optional)
- writes a concluding comment that contains evaluative comment and summarises aspects of the recount

Language Features
- writes about specific participants
- writes cohesively using a variety of linking words to do with time, e.g. *next, after, subsequently, the following day, meanwhile*
- uses a variety of sentence beginnings to make the recount more interesting
- maintains simple past tense or manipulates tense

Sample of Recount writing:

When	Who	Where	What	Why	Feelings
Yesterday after school at 4 o'clock	Me and Naomi	at Naomi's house	play on the swing, volley ball.	Because I was inzited to Naomi's	I Felt very happy

My News Plan

Yesterday after school at 4 o clock I went to Naomi's house to play. Naomi and I played volley ball over the bars. After a while we got bored so we went on the swing. Naomi and I turned the swing around and around. Naomi got on the swing then I pushed her. It spiraled in a forward motion. It was fun. Then I went home.

Early Writing Phase Indicators from Writing: Developmental Continuum highlighted:

The writer:

◆ **uses a small range of familiar text forms**
◆ **chooses topics that are personally significant**
• often writes a simple recount of personal events or observation and comment
• uses time order to sequence and organise writing
• writes simple factual accounts with little elaboration
◆ **uses basic sentence structures and varies sentence beginnings**
◆ **can explain in context, some of the purposes of using writing, e.g. shopping list or telephone messages as a memory aid**
◆ **experiments with words drawn from language experience activities, literature, media and oral language of peers and others**
◆ **attempts to use some punctuation**
• sometimes uses full stops
• sometimes uses a capital letter to start a sentence
• uses capital letters for names
• attempts to transfer knowledge of text structure to writing, e.g. imitates form of a familiar big book
◆ **talks with others to plan and revise own writing**
• shares ideas for writing with peers or teacher

Recount Continuum Indicators (Developing) highlighted:

The writer:

• uses recounts to reconstruct past events
• establishes time, place and participants of recount and includes events in sequence
• writes additional information about more important events, e.g. 'My dad took me to the zoo. I saw all the animals. The elephant was the biggest and best animal. I liked the monkeys too. When it was dark, we went home.'
• includes only characters of significance to the recount
• writes a satisfactory conclusion
• begins to use structures of written language
• uses some adverbs and adjectives to clarify meaning
• maintains tense
• uses action verbs and generally shows agreement between subject and verb, e.g. *I went, I saw, I did*
• writes complete sentences

This page provides an example of the combined use of the *Writing: Developmental Continuum* and the continuum for Recount writing, to evaluate a sample of writing. It confirms placement on the *Writing: Developmental Continuum* and can be used to assess control of Recount writing.

Sample of Recount writing:

Our Visit to an Ice Cream Factory

Yesterday the children from Room 10 went by bus to Peters ice cream factory in Balcatta to find out how ice cream was made.

When we arrived we all got a free hat and then watched a video about making ice cream. The lady showed us some new products and some people were allowed to taste them I didn't like the Green Tea ice cream at all!

After the video session we split into two groups and a lady showed us around the factory and explained how ice cream was made. It was quite interesting to look through the windows but we couldn't get near the ice creams. I found out that Peters export a lot of ice cream to Asian and other countries.

Before we left we went to the cafeteria and were allowed to choose a free ice cream. We all sat on the lawn and ate it. My ice cream was a chocolate drumstick it was delicious.

As soon as everyone had finished eating we got on the bus and went back to school.

Conventional Writing Phase Indicators from Writing: Developmental Continuum highlighted:

The writer:

- ◆ **uses text forms to suit purpose and audience**
- • takes account of some aspects of context, purpose and audience
- • considers the needs of audience and includes background information
- ◆ **can explain why some text form may be more appropriate than another to achieve a specific purpose**
- • demonstrates the ability to develop a topic
- ◆ **uses a variety of simple, compound and extended sentences**
- ◆ **groups sentences containing related information into paragraphs**
- • orders ideas in time order or other sequence such as priority order
- • uses a variety of linking words such as *and, so, because, if, next, after, before, first*
- ◆ **is beginning to select vocabulary according to the demands of audience and purpose, e.g. uses subject-specific vocabulary**
- ◆ **uses proof reading guide or checklist to edit own or peers' writing**
- ◆ **punctuates simple sentences correctly**
- • uses capital letters for proper nouns
- • uses capital letters to start sentences
- • uses capital letters for titles
- • uses full stops to end sentences
- ◆ **uses a range of strategies for planning, revising and publishing own written texts**
- • plans writing using notes, lists or diagrams or other relevant information

Recount Continuum Indicators (Consolidating) highlighted:

The Writer:

- • demonstrates understanding that recounts can retell a personal experience, record particulars of an event, e.g. a football match, be an imaginative description of events
- • demonstrates understanding that diaries, news reports, biographies, journals, may be recounts
- • provides an orientation that is complete and succinct and includes significant events in chronological sequence
- • caters for reader by providing contextual details
- • attempts to interpret events imaginatively, elaborating important events
- • sustains topic throughout
- • maintains consistent past tense
- • varies conjunctions and linking words to indicate time, e.g. *soon, later, eventually*
- • writes complete sentences that are increasingly complex
- • groups sentences containing related information into paragraphs

This page provides an example of the combined use of the *Writing: Developmental Continuum* and the continuum for Recount writing, to evaluate a sample of writing. It confirms placement on the *Writing: Developmental Continuum* and can be used to assess control of Recount writing.

CHECKLIST FOR RECOUNTS	ALWAYS	SOMETIMES	NOT YET

Purpose:

The writer:
- demonstrates understanding that recounts can be written for a number of purposes and audiences and that a writer's experiences influence what he/she writes

Text Organisation and Content
- organises the schematic structure of the recount by starting with an orientation that aims to interest the reader and including important events relating to a particular occasion

Orientation
- includes all relevant background information needed to understand the text, i.e. who was involved, when and where it happened and other pertinent details

Events
- develops the topic fully by including significant events chosen to add interest and impact
- elaborates events so that the reader is able to visualise the experience
- interprets events imaginatively, symbolically or metaphorically
- orders the events chronologically into easily followed sequential steps
- sometimes includes personal reflections or comments about events in the recount, e.g. it was a great honour...

Evaluation (optional)
- writes a concluding comment that contains evaluative comment and summarises aspects of the recount

Language Features
- writes about specific participants
- writes cohesively using a variety of linking words to do with time, e.g. *next, after, subsequently, the following day, meanwhile*
- uses a variety of sentence beginnings to make the recount more interesting
- maintains simple past tense or manipulates tense

Chapter 5:

Procedures

Procedural texts follow a discernible pattern—listing sequences of actions or steps to show the way to do something. Procedural texts can be oral or written.

Features of Procedures

Purpose
The purpose of a procedure is to deal with the general way to do things.

Focus
A procedural text is composed of ordered sequences.

Types
Procedural texts play a big part in our everyday life and are used in many contexts. The purpose and audience will dictate the level of technical language used and the way in which the information is organised. Some texts may tell how something is done. These include recipes, science experiments, maths procedures, *How to play* …, *How to make a* …, and *How to do it* manuals. Others give instructions for how to use or operate things like appliances and machines. There are many procedural texts used and they all aim to get things done.

Examples
Procedures may be used in many areas of the curriculum, e.g.

English	How to organise an essay
Social Studies	How to use an atlas to locate a place
Maths	How to find the perimeter of a rectangle using 1 cm cubes
Health	How to treat snake bite
Science	How to conduct an experiment
Physical Education	How to play a game

Text Organisation
A procedure generally has four components. Each stage has a separate and distinct function.

The first is the **Goal** or **Aim** that states what is to be done. It may outline the situation which has arisen and requires an ordered procedure for resolution.

This is followed by a list of **Materials** or **Requirements**. These are listed in order of use and include items needed to complete the specific task :

* tools, instruments, utensils
* ingredients, materials, parts, data.

The **_Method_** is then presented as a series of steps. These may be abbreviated or tabulated as in a recipe, or presented as connected sentences or paragraphs.

The final step in a procedural text is the **_Evaluation_**. (This is sometimes omitted.) It states how the success of the procedure can be tested or evaluated.

Headings, subheadings, numbered steps, diagrams, photographs, etc. are often used to help clarify instructions so that they are easily followed.

Framework headings may vary in different contexts, e.g.

A **Science experiment** might have:
Aim / Goal / Hypothesis
Equipment
Procedure
Observations
Conclusion

Instructions to play a game could include:
How to win / goal of the game
Number of players
Equipment
Rules of the game
How to score

Recipes would need:
Name of the food to be cooked
Utensils and ingredients
Method

Machinery manuals often have:
Operation to be completed, e.g. How to start your …
Warnings for safe operation, e.g. Before you start make sure that…
Steps to follow including detailed, labelled diagrams of relevant parts
Evaluation and alternatives, e.g. If the monitor remains blank…

Different contexts will require different framework headings but the overall structure is the same.

Language Features

- Generalised participants referring to a whole class of things (ingredients, utensils) as well as specific ones (the eggs)
- The reader or the person following the instructions is referred to in a general way (one/you) or sometimes is not even mentioned at all (Draw a 10cm line)
- Linking words to do with time (first, then, when)
- Mainly action verbs (material processes); (put, twist, hold, take)
- Tense is timeless (what people do in general), e.g. simple present tense (you stir, you cut, you mix)
- Detailed, factual description of participants (shapes, size, colour, amount, etc.)
- Detailed information on how (carefully, with the knife, quickly); where (6cm from the top, into the bowl, in the oven); when (after you have folded the serviette)

(Adapted from Derewianka B. 1990, *Exploring How Texts Work*, pp. 27-28.)

PROCEDURE

PROCEDURE

- **Goal/Aim**
  - What is to be done?
- **Requirements**
  - What is needed to complete this task?
    - a) tools, instruments, utensils...
    - b) data, ingredients, parts...
- **Steps**
  - First step to last step
  - a) What is to be done?
  - b) How is it to be done?
- **Evaluation/Testing**
  - Was the goal achieved?

Procedure Framework

Replacement of batteries in the XYZ calculator.

When the calculator fails to show a lighted display or does not compute correctly, the batteries are run down and must be replaced. The following procedure will result in the correct installation of new batteries.

In order to complete the battery installation, a small Phillips screwdriver is required. Two new AAA size batteries should be used.

The following steps are implemented:

1. Undo the two screws in the back of the calculator.
2. Take off the back cover.
3. Remove the old batteries and replace with the new batteries.
4. Replace the back cover of the calculator.
5. Insert and tighten the two screws.

Turn the calculator on and test the display and the accuracy of the computation.

Title summarises goal

Detailed factual description of components

Replacement of Batteries in the XYZ Calculator

When the calculator fails to show a lighted display, or does not compute correctly, the batteries are run down and must ← Goal be replaced. The following procedure will result in the correct installation of new batteries.

Timeless present tense

In order to complete the battery installation, a small Phillips screwdriver is required. Two new AAA size batteries should ← Requirements be used.

No reference made to reader

The following steps are implemented: ⟵———— Method
1. <u>Undo</u> the two screws in the back of the calculator.
2. <u>Take off</u> the back cover.
3. <u>Remove</u> the old batteries and replace with the new batteries.
4. <u>Replace</u> the back cover of the calculator.
5. <u>Insert</u> and tighten the two screws.

Action verbs often begin each sentence

Turn the calculator on and test the display and the accuracy ← Evaluation of the computation.

Framework and text written by Dr Peter Sloan and Dr Ross Latham for the First Steps Project.

Replacement of Batteries in the XYZ Calculator

When the calculator fails to show a lighted display or does not compute correctly, the batteries are run down and must be replaced. The following procedure will result in the correct installation of new batteries.

In order to complete the battery installation, a small Phillips screwdriver is required. Two new AAA size batteries should be used.

The following steps are implemented:

1. Undo the two screws in the back of the calculator.
2. Take off the back cover.
3. Remove the old batteries and replace with the new batteries.
4. Replace the back cover of the calculator.
5. Insert and tighten the two screws.

Turn the calculator on and test the display and the accuracy of the computation.

This simple text has the structural and linguistic features of common procedures and it may be used for analysis. See activities on page 73.

Written by Dr Peter Sloan and Dr Ross Latham for the First Steps Project.

Exploring and Planning Procedures

The following suggestions may be used by teachers to introduce procedures orally and informally to Role Play and Experimental Phase writers.

Oral sharing

Class recipe books

Draw and label

Early, Conventional and Proficient Phase writers will benefit from some of the following activities.

Role play and interview

Collect and analyse

Text reconstruction

Direct model

A problem-solving approach

Joint construction

Independent construction

Activities

Oral Sharing

Children are often involved in making things and can be encouraged to explain what they have made and how they made it during oral sharing time or sharing circles. Children may start with simple labelling and a general description, e.g. *I made a boat and it's made of boxes*. Teachers may need to model explaining how the work was produced. Questioning can also be used to guide children. e.g.

Can you tell us what things you used to make it?
What was the first thing you had to do?
What did you do after that?
If you had to explain to someone who hadn't done something like this before, what is the main thing you would tell them to remember?

Positive comments about children's efforts will help them focus on improving their instructions. e.g.

I liked the way Sam told us all the steps in order.
I liked the way Dillon told us exactly what materials he needed so we can get the same things when we make it.

Class Recipe Books

Modelling procedures that are relevant to children will help them understand the purpose and form of written instructions. Teachers can record making and doing activities in big books (written by teacher as children watch). These class experience books are popular with young children as they provide a shared language for reading and a stimulus for writing. Even children who cannot read and write for themselves feel they can manage these texts. The books should be placed alongside commercial publications and occasionally referred to, e.g.

Do you remember when we made pikelets? What did we need? Let's look in our class recipe book and check. Oh yes, …

Next week we will be making pancakes. They are nearly the same. I'll write the recipe on the next page and then we can buy the ingredients.

The same idea can be used to record other instructions in separate books. Children will need diagrams and pictures to help them follow the instructions.

Draw and Label

Model the use of drawing and labelling the steps involved in a procedure. e.g. if you are going to germinate seeds as part of a class topic draw a pot, potting mix, packet of seeds and watering can in the first frame and label them Materials. Draw and label each step involved in planting seeds. Ask children to follow the instructions to plant their seeds.

Early, Conventional and Proficient Phase writers will be writing procedural texts in a number of different curriculum areas. The overall structure will remain the same but there may be different headings, e.g. Utensils / Equipment, Ingredients / Materials to suit particular contexts. The following ideas will help them explore and control this type of writing to suit particular purposes and audiences.

Role Play and Interview

Children act the role of the 'maker' and the 'interviewer' and ask questions using the procedural text framework headings as a guide to compose questions.

Collect and Analyse

Ask children to collect procedures of the particular type they are going to write, e.g. a collection of recipes, game instructions or how to make craft objects etc.

In groups or as a whole class children compile a list of common elements of each procedure. Discuss headings, format and language used. Children then devise their own rules for writing their procedures.

Encourage children to place their procedures in class collections for future use. Make sure that these collections (loose leaf files) are available for children to take home and use, e.g. *Our Class Cookbook*—recipes, *Our Book of Games* —game instructions, *Our Things to Make Book*—craft ideas. Children can add to these collections when they wish.

Direct Model

Use overhead projector to display a procedure (such as sample text Replacement of Batteries in the XYZ Calculator page 71). Ask questions of each paragraph. Students work together to build up framework headings and understanding of the content. Attach framework labels e.g.

| Title | Briefly tells the reader what the instructions are for Sometimes the title is the goal, e.g. recipes) |

Paragraph 1
What is the purpose?   To tell what is to be done.

What can we call it?

| Aim or goal |

Paragraph 2

What is the purpose?   To tell what we need to do the job.

What could we call it?

> | Requirements |

Paragraph 3

What is the purpose?   It's a list of steps to take to do the job

What could we call it?

> | Method |

Paragraph 4

What is the purpose?   To test it and see if it works.

What could we call it?

> | Evaluation |

Chart the features and the guiding questions so that children can use the framework headings to jointly construct a relevant procedural text and try their text by giving it to a classmate to follow.

Text Reconstruction

Children reconstruct a procedural text from jumbled paragraphs. They discuss clues used to reassemble the text.

Exploring Procedures—a problem-solving approach

A problem solving approach to teaching writing of procedures is an effective way to help Early, Conventional and Proficient Phase writers to improve their written procedures.

Use shared reading sessions to show students different types of procedural texts. Talk about the purposes of procedural texts and who might use them.

The 'Pikelets' texts following can be used as a starting point for children to discuss procedures if they are going to be writing recipes. The framework they devise can be used, or adapted, for writing any recipe.

The sample texts are from a year two/three class and were collected before any discussions about recipe writing. The children were asked to write how they had made pikelets so they could take the instructions home and try the recipe. Some children had little experience of cooking and using recipe books, others had participated in cooking both at home and at school. Their writing reflects their experiences (as it so often does).

SAMPLE 1
Pikelets

Flour
Carb Soda
Sugar
Egg
sour milk
butter

Sift the first two things into a bowl.

Put the other things in. You have to melt the butter first. Mix it all up.

Cook the pikelets in a hot frying pan. Eat them hot or cold with butter.

SAMPLE 2
We made some pikelets

Today in Room 7 we made pikelets. We all had a turn at sifting the flour and carb soda. I put the sugar in Angela put the egg in and Joel put the milk in. We all stirred it but Joel knocked over the bowl and some of the stuff spilt out. I cleaned up the mess. When it was mixed we poured in some melted butter and mixed it up. We cooked the pikelets and ate them.

They were yummy!!

SAMPLE 3
Pikelets

Ingredients:

1 cup self-raising flour

1/2 teaspoon carb soda

2 tablespoons sugar

1 egg

1/2 cup sour milk

60 grams butter

Method:

1. Sift together, flour and carb. soda.
2. Add egg, milk and sugar.
3. Mix.
4. Pour in melted butter.
5. Mix.
6. Place by spoonful into hot pan (160°C).
7. Cook until bubbling.
8. Turn to brown other side.

SAMPLE 4
How to make pikelets

Instructions

You have to get a cup of self raising flour and 1/2 teaspoon of carb soda and sift them into a bowl. Then you have to put in one egg, 2 tablespoons of sugar and 1/2 a cup of sour milk and stir the mixture up so it looks not lumpy. You have to melt the butter and mix it with the other stuff.

You heat the electric frying pan and put a spoonful in each corner. When you have cooked the pikelets they taste great. I like to eat the mixture before it cooks.

Read the Pikelets texts and talk with students asking them to decide which text would be the best to have if you wanted to make pikelets.

The following text is an excerpt from year 3/4 children who were involved in discussion about the texts.

Students said:
I think number 2 isn't a recipe because it just tells about the day. It doesn't even tell how much of each ingredients are needed.
Teacher wrote:
No information about ingredients.

Students said:
You shouldn't write about spilling stuff because that isn't anything to do with how to make pikelets.
Teacher wrote:
Irrelevant information included.

Students said:
Number 1 is set out clearly but there are no amounts in it and the method is jumbled.
Teacher wrote:
Steps not in order. No exact quantities.

Students said:
Number 4 is hard to follow although the information is all there.
Teacher wrote:
Information isn't easy to find.

Students said:
It says 'you' all the time. That isn't necessary because the reader knows it means him/her.
Teacher wrote:
'You' can be deleted as it is implied by the writer and not needed by the reader.

Students said:
Number 3 is the best. It has a title.
Teacher wrote:
Title tells what is to be made.

Students said:
It lists the amount and name of each ingredient.
Teacher wrote:
Ingredients and amounts are listed clearly.

Students said:
The instructions are short and clear

and it doesn't include unnecessary details.
Teacher wrote:
Instructions are in order and contain detailed information that helps the user.

Students said:
The instructions start with a thing to do,
not with you all the time.
Teacher wrote:
The reader is not usually referred to. In the method section sentences often start with a verb.

The children continued to work through the samples making comparisons and comments which the teacher jotted down. The comments they made indicated that they already had ideas about how procedural texts should be constructed. The children reviewed their information and constructed their 'Rules for Writing Recipes Chart.'

Joint Construction

Before children were asked to compose their own text the teacher demonstrated how to write a make believe recipe during a shared writing session. Children contributed suggestions.

When constructing a procedural text (e.g. a recipe) include these points:
- write a succinct title
- include utensils and exact ingredients required in list form
- in the method section:
  - make sure that each step is numbered and clearly stated in the correct order
  - use action verbs, e.g. mix, add, stir
  - include detailed information by adding a precise adverb, e.g. Quickly add…
  - talk about excluding the pronoun 'you' because it is unnecessary
  - use simple present tense, e.g. stir, add, mix, place

Independent Construction

This followed another cooking session so that children could use the recipe at home.

During science and art the children wrote different procedural texts to consolidate their understanding of the form. Children needed to adjust the framework to suit the purpose and audience but the main features remained the same.

Evaluation

After writing children were encouraged to evaluate the effectiveness of their writing by checking with their Procedure Chart and then trying out their instructions on other people to see if all information was included.

Planning Frameworks

Encourage children to use planning frameworks (see pages 78–9) to outline procedures.

PROCEDURE PLAN

TOPIC: _____

AIM:
What is to be done?
REQUIREMENTS:
What is needed?
METHOD:
What is to be done? 1. 2. 3. 4. 5. 6.
Was goal achieved?

PROCEDURE PLAN

Write information in each section.

TOPIC: _____

GOAL/AIM:

What is to be done?

REQUIREMENTS:

What is needed to complete this task?

(a) tools, instruments, utensils...

(b) ingredients, parts, material

METHOD:

What is to be done?

EVALUATION/TESTING:

Was the goal achieved?

Assessment and Evaluation of Procedure Writing

The indicators on the following page trace the development of Procedure writing. Teachers may wish to use the indicators to assess children's control of Procedure writing.

Samples of the combined use of the *Writing: Developmental Continuum* and the continuum for Procedure writing are included on pages 82–3 to show how teachers use a combination of both to evaluate children's writing. It is suggested that samples of work be examined and indicators highlighted. The information provided forms a basis for teaching and enables teachers to help children see how their writing can be improved.

A checklist for Procedures is provided on page 84. This is made up of the indicators for the Extending stage of Procedure writing and can be used as a quick way of assessing children's progress in writing Procedural texts.

PROCEDURE INDICATORS

BEGINNING

Purpose:
The writer:
- discusses the use of simple procedures such as recipes

Text Organisation
- writes observation and comment or a recount

Goal
- briefly mentions goal, e.g. 'This is how you make a cake'

Materials
- mentions some materials

Method
- requires help to include all steps of procedure in correct sequence
- illustrates steps of procedure
- uses labels or captions for illustrations of procedure

Language Features
- uses language close to speech, e.g. 'The first thing you do is put an egg in.'
- links steps using 'and then'
- uses generalised 'you', e.g. 'you put some bananas in then you mash them'

DEVELOPING

Purpose:
The writer:
- discusses the purpose and advantage of written instructions

Text Organisation and Content
- uses a procedure framework

Goal
- states purpose or goal

Materials
- lists materials required

Method
- includes most of the necessary steps of procedure in sequence
- illustrates to support text

Language Features
- maintains simple present tense throughout
- uses linking words to signal time, e.g. *first, when, then, after*
- omits 'you' and starts sentences with a verb or adverb, e.g. *Stir, Add, Cut, Carefully glue*
- uses action verbs

CONSOLIDATING

Purpose:
The writer:
- can identify and describe a range of purposes for written procedures

Text Organisation and Content
- structures text using or adapting a procedure framework

Goal
- states goal precisely

Materials
- lists materials required, under a heading
- shows some evidence of appropriate layout

Method
- states method or instruction in correct sequence with adequate detail
- uses diagrams to support text

Language Features
- writes referring to classes of things (ingredients; equipment) as well as specific ones (the flour, the salt)
- refers to reader in general way (one/you) or does not mention the reader (turn the handle, add the water)
- maintains simple present tense throughout
- develops coherence through use of linking words such as *after, next, while, during, secondly, finally*
- uses subject-specific vocabulary
- includes some explanations to justify results

EXTENDING

Purpose:
The writer:
- demonstrates understanding of a large range of contexts where written procedures may be used to tell how to do or make something
- accurately interprets need of the audience by identifying and including relevant information in written procedures

Text Organisation and Content
- selects and uses an appropriate procedure framework for different contexts
- uses layout that is appropriate to the subject and topic

Goal
- states goal using precise terminology appropriate to the context and form

Materials
- clearly lists all materials and quantities required

Method
- writes explicit instructions for sequence of steps required to complete task
- includes detailed information on 'how', 'where' and 'when' each step is to be completed
- uses diagrams, photographs, illustrations to elaborate and support text where appropriate
- evaluates outcome (optional)

Language Features
- uses procedural order to provide text cohesion
- uses appropriate terminology
- uses linking words to do with time, e.g. *first, next, after ten minutes*
- guides reader accurately by use of precise adverbs or adjectives, e.g. *slowly unwind the larger spool, carefully cut a 10cm wide strip from the left side*
- uses simple present tense, e.g. *stir the mixture until it boils*
- refers to the reader in a general way or not at all, e.g. 'you mix', 'one mixes', or 'mix'
- selects appropriate headings for stages of procedure according to context and purpose, e.g. Goal/Aim/Hypothesis, Utensils/Equipment/Ingredients.

Sample of Procedure writing:

> # Wednesday June 3th
>
> This is How You Make a Cake. Fast Thing You do is You Put Some egg. The Sekan Thing Youdo is You Put Some fluwe. Then the ^ thad Thing You Put is Some Bananas Then You Mes It all UP. Then You Put It in the uvan

Early Writing Phase Indicators from Writing: Developmental Continuum highlighted:

The writer:

- ◆ **uses a small range of familiar text forms**
- ◆ **chooses topics that are personally significant**
- • uses time order to sequence and organise writing
- • is beginning to use some informational text structures, e.g. recipes, factual description
- ◆ **uses basic sentence structures and varies sentence beginnings**
- ◆ **can explain in context, some of he purposes of using writing, e.g. shopping list or telephone messages as a memory aid**
- ◆ experiments with words drawn from language experience activities, literature, media and oral language of peers and others
- ◆ **begins to develop editing skills**
- • adds words to clarify meaning
- • begins to proof read for spelling errors
- ◆ **attempts to use some punctuation**
- • sometimes uses full stops
- • sometimes uses a capital letter to start a sentence
- ◆ **talks with others to plan and revise own writing**

Procedure Continuum Indicators (Beginning) highlighted:

The writer:

- • discusses the use of simple procedures such as recipes
- • writes observation and comment or a recount
- • briefly mentions goal
- • requires help to include all steps of procedure in correct sequence
- • uses language close to speech, e.g. 'The first thing you do is put an egg in.'
- • uses generalised 'you', e.g. 'you put some bananas in then you mash them'

This page provides an example of the combined used of the *Writing: Developmental Continuum* and the continuum for Procedure writing, to evaluate a sample of writing. It confirms placement on the *Writing: Developmental Continuum* and can be used to assess control of Procedure writing.

Sample of Procedure writing:

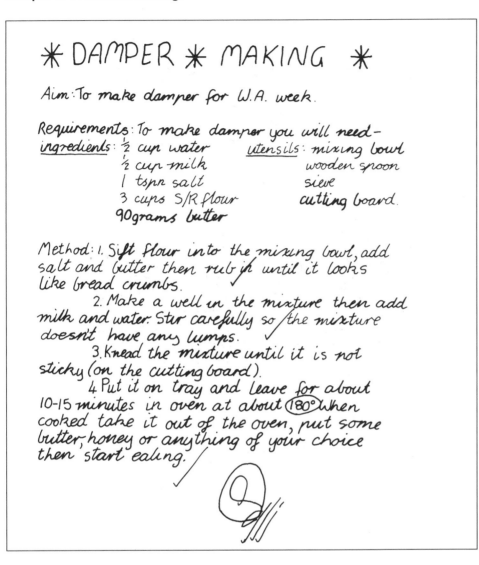

> # * DAMPER * MAKING *
>
> Aim: To make damper for W.A. week.
>
> Requirements: To make damper you will need —
> <u>ingredients</u>: ½ cup water   <u>utensils</u>: mixing bowl
>   ½ cup milk   wooden spoon
>   1 tspn salt   sieve
>   3 cups S/R flour   cutting board.
>   90grams butter
>
> Method: 1. Sift flour into the mixing bowl, add salt and butter then rub in until it looks like bread crumbs.
>   2. Make a well in the mixture then add milk and water. Stir carefully so the mixture doesn't have any lumps. ✓
>   3. Knead the mixture until it is not sticky (on the cutting board).
>   4 Put it on tray and leave for about 10-15 minutes in oven at about (180°) When cooked take it out of the oven, put some butter, honey or anything of your choice then start eating. ✓

Conventional Writing Phase Indicators from Writing: Developmental Continuum highlighted:

The writer:

- **uses text forms to suit purpose and audience**
- **can explain why some text form may be more appropriate than another to achieve a specific purpose**
- **writes a range of texts forms including stories, reports, procedures and expositions**
- **uses a variety of simple, compound and extended sentences**
- **groups sentences containing related information into paragraphs**
- **is beginning to select vocabulary according to the demands of audience and purpose, e.g. uses subject-specific vocabulary**
- **uses proof reading guide or checklist to edit own or peers' writing**
- **punctuates simple sentences correctly**
- **uses a range of strategies for planning, revising and publishing own written texts**

Procedure Continuum Indicators (Consolidating) highlighted:

The writer:

- can identify and describe a range of purposes for written procedures
- structures text using or adapting a procedure framework
- states goal precisely
- lists materials required, under a heading
- shows some evidence of appropriate layout
- states method or instruction in correct sentence with adequate detail
- writes referring to classes of things (ingredients, equipment) as well as specific ones (the flour, the salt)
- refers to reader in general way (one/you) or does not mention the reader (turn the handle, add the water)
- maintains simple present tense throughout
- develops coherence through use of linking words such as *after, next, while, during, secondly, finally*
- uses subject-specific vocabulary

This page provides an example of the combined used of the *Writing: Developmental Continuum* and the continuum for Procedure writing, to evaluate a sample of writing. It confirms placement on the *Writing: Developmental Continuum* and can be used to assess control of Procedure writing.

CHECKLIST FOR PROCEDURAL TEXT	ALWAYS	SOMETIMES	NOT YET

Purpose:

The writer:
- demonstrates understanding of a large range of contexts where written procedures may be used to tell how to do or make something
- accurately interprets need of the audience by identifying and including relevant information in written procedures

Text Organisation and Content
- selects and uses an appropriate procedure framework for different contexts
- uses layout that is appropriate to the subject and topic

Goal
- states goal using precise terminology appropriate to the context and form

Materials
- clearly lists all materials and quantities required

Method
- writes explicit instructions for sequence of steps required to complete task
- includes detailed information on 'how', 'where' and 'when' each step is to be completed
- uses diagrams, photographs, illustrations to elaborate and support text where appropriate
- evaluates outcome (optional)

Language Features
- uses procedural order to provide text cohesion
- uses appropriate terminology
- uses linking words to do with time, e.g. *first, next, after ten minutes*
- guides reader accurately by use of precise adverbs or adjectives, e.g. *slowly unwind the larger spool, carefully cut a 10cm wide strip from the left side*
- uses simple present tense, e.g. *stir the mixture until it boils*
- refers to the reader in a general way or not at all, e.g. 'you mix', 'one mixes', or 'mix'
- selects appropriate headings for stages of procedure according to context and purpose, e.g. Goal/Aim/ Hypothesis, Utensils/Equipment/Ingredients.

Chapter 6:

Reports

Reports are factual texts that present information clearly and succinctly. The stages of a report are context-specific and relate very closely to its purpose. A Report about Reptiles would begin with a classification and go on describe particular aspects such as appearance, location and dynamics. Whereas, a Report on Pioneer Women may classify them into privileged, working class and convicts and go on to describe and compare aspects such as social status, housing and health. Both texts would be classified as reports but the stages or organising framework would differ.

Features of Reports

Purpose

The purpose of a report is to systematically organise and record factual information to classify and describe a whole class of things.

Focus

General things

Types

There are many contexts in which people are asked to write 'reports', e.g. eyewitness reports, newspaper reports, progress reports. Many of these could, however, be more accurately described as another form such as a recount. In this book Reports refer to factual texts that classify and describe a class of things.

Examples

Reports may be written in all curriculum areas, e.g.
A Report on Deserts
A Report on Heart Disease
A Report on Birds
A Report on Life in the 1920's after reading *My Place*
A Report on Computers

Text Organisation

A report usually introduces the topic with an opening **Generalisation** or **Classification**. This may be in the form of a definition (e.g. Snakes are reptiles) or a reference to the particular aspect of the topic to be elaborated in the report, (e.g. There are many poisonous snakes in Australia).

This is followed by a **Description** of various aspects of the topic. Aspects described will vary according to the context of the report, e.g. if the report were dealing with a class of animals, aspects such as physical characteristics, location and dynamics would be elaborated. However, if the topic were computers, components and their function might be described.

Reports often conclude with a **Summarising Comment**.

Language Features

- Generalised participants: a whole class of things (e.g. volcanoes, newspapers, the royal family) rather than specific participants (Mt Vesuvius, The Times, Queen Elizabeth)
- Some action verbs (material processes) especially when describing behaviour (climb, eat , erupt)
- Many 'linking' verbs (relational processes), (is, are, have, belongs to)
- Usually in timeless present tense (are, exist, grow)
- Descriptive language, but factual and precise rather than imaginative
- Language for defining, classifying, comparing and contrasting (are called, belong to, can be classified as, are similar to, are more powerful than)
- Likely to contain technical vocabulary
- The writing is in a relatively formal objective style. The use of first person pronouns (I, we) and the writer's opinions are not generally appropriate to this type of writing

(Adapted from Derewianka B. 1990 *Exploring How Texts Work*, p. 53)

REPORT

The Honey Bee

The honey bee is an insect.

The honey bee is bright yellow and orange. It is 12mm long and has six legs. The honey bee has three separate parts to its body.

This insect lives in all parts of Australia.

These bees collect nectar for honey. They dance on the honeycomb to show the other bees where the best flowers for honey are. Honey bees may fly 20,000 km to collect enough nectar for 500 g of honey.

Most people like the honey that the bees work so hard to make.

REPORT

- Classification or Generalisation
  - What is the focus?
- Description
  - What are the important features to be elaborated?
- Summarising Comment

Report Framework

Generalised participants - a class of things

Linking verbs - is a, has,
Action verbs - collect, dance, fly, work

Demonstrative pronouns direct attention to the nouns

Timeless present tense

The Honey Bee

The honey bee is an insect.

The honey bee is bright yellow and orange. It is 12mm long and has six legs. The honey bee has three separate parts to its body.

This insect lives in all parts of Australia.

These bees collect nectar for honey. They dance on the honeycomb to show the other bees where the best flowers for honey are. Honey bees may fly 20,000km to collect enough nectar for 500g of honey.

Most people like the honey that the bees work so hard to make.

Classification

Description
* What it looks like.

* Where it lives.

* What it does.

Summarising Comment

* Aspects of the description vary according to the context of the Report

Framework and text written by Dr Peter Sloan and Dr Ross Latham for the First Steps Project.

THE HONEY BEE

The honey bee is an insect.

The honey bee is bright yellow and orange. It is 12mm long and has six legs. The honey bee has three separate parts to its body.

This insect lives in all parts of Australia.

These bees collect nectar for honey. They dance on the honeycomb to show the other bees where the best flowers for honey are. Honey bees may fly 20,000km to collect enough nectar for 500g of honey.

Most people like the honey that the bees work so hard to make.

This simple text has the structural and linguistic features of common reports and it may be used for analysis. See activities on page 94.

Written by Dr Peter Sloan and Dr Ross Latham for the First Steps Project.

Exploring and Planning Reports

Reports are commonly used in Science and Social Studies but preparation for written reports starts long before children are required to write them. Children start describing and classifying familiar items at home and so from kindergarten on, activities can be provided to extend the vocabulary and classification skills necessary for moving into report writing. This is done orally and informally, e.g. teacher questions about chickens hatched in the classroom will help lay the foundation for written reports.

What are they?
What do they look like?
What do they eat?
How do they move?

Activities

There are a number of different methods of helping students to investigate reports. Each method can be adapted to suit the demands of different children. The following ideas can be used for writing or pre-writing workshops.

For Role Play and Experimental writers:

Show and tell

What am I?

Classification activities

Shared reading

For Early, Conventional and Proficient writers:

Random fact sheet

Direct model

Problem solving

Retrieval chart

Show and Tell

A show and tell chart with guiding questions will help children describe articles they bring for news. e.g.

What is it called?
What does it look like?
Where did you get it?
What does it do?

What Am I?

Display objects or pictures. Instruct one child to choose an item and give clues or answer questions to help the group guess its identity. Use a description framework to guide children if necessary, e.g.

What kind of thing is it? (a toy, an animal)
What does it look like? (colour, size, shape, weight)
Where is kept? (at home, on the table)
What can it do? (write, fix things)

Classification Activities

Sorting, pattern making and grouping activities provide excellent opportunities for developing children's precise descriptive language. Teacher facilitation will help children to focus on the unique and shared characteristics of objects and help them to develop and refine ways of talking about the features they observe.

Shared Reading

Use shared reading sessions to show students how an information text differs from a narrative text. Introduce non-fiction books related to topics being studied and indicate important features and conventions used in this type of text.

Mention the Table of Contents, Index, Glossary, headings, subheadings, use of photographs and diagrams to support the text, the type of language used and the layout of the text.

Talk about the purpose of a report and what the author needed to know before writing the text. Model how to find information, pointing out that information texts do not have to be read from cover to cover.

Discuss some of the following :

Why did the author choose this format for the book?
What did the author have to know to write this book?
Why are headings and subheadings used?
What can you say about the use of diagrams, photos, drawings in the book?
What sort of information is likely to be presented in this way?
When would we want to write in this way?
What did you learn from this book?

Random Fact Sheet

Early Writers often need help with organising information into paragraphs. Report writing using a *random fact sheet* has been successful with many children. The procedures beginning on page 91 can be adapted for different topics.

RANDOM FACT SHEET

Objective: to classify information

During modelled writing session class brainstorm to produce a random list of facts about the topic.

FACTS ABOUT DROMORNIS

1   heaviest bird ever known
2   lived in beech forests
3   bones/fossils found—Alice Springs, Northern Territory
4   related to emus
5   full name Dromornis stirtoni
6   three metres high
7   weighed as much as a small car
8   like giant emu
9   very thick legs
10 could not fly
11 food—plants
12 a bird
13 toes like hooves
14 lived prehistoric times—now extinct
15 related to cassowaries
16 lived 15 million years ago
17 three toes
18 scaly neck
19 long, coarse, black feathers
20 large, strong beak
21 hunted on forest floor

PLANNING SHEET

Children then suggest how facts can be clustered into categories and suggest a name for each category, e.g. Classification, Description, Time/place, Dynamics

Classification

full name Dromornis stirtoni
related to emus
a bird
related to cassowaries
extinct—lived prehistoric times

Time/Place

lived in beech forests
bones/fossils found—Alice Springs, NT
lived 15 million years ago

Description

heaviest bird ever known
weighed as much as small car
like giant emu
very thick legs
toes like hooves
three toes
scaly neck
long, coarse, black feathers
large, strong beak
three metres high

Dynamics

could not fly
food—plants
hunted on forest floor

Written by Dr Peter Sloan and Dr Ross Latham for the First Steps Project.

Objective: To jointly construct a report using information from research.

Teacher models how to expand facts into sentences and write a first draft to include facts under category headings.

Classification:
Dromornis stirtoni was a bird. Dromornis was related to emus and cassowaries. Dromornis is an extinct bird.

Description:
Dromornis was the heaviest bird ever known. Dromornis weighed as much as a small car. It had very thick legs. It had long, coarse, black feathers. It had three toes. Dromornis's toes were like hooves. Dromornis was three metres high. It had a large, strong beak. Dromornis looked like a giant emu.

Time/Place:
Dromornis lived 15 million years ago. It lived in the beech forests of Australia. Its fossils were found near Alice Springs in the Northern Territory.

Dynamics:
Dromornis could not fly. It hunted on the forest floor. It ate plants.

Ending Comment:
Dromornis must have been a fearsome sight.

Written by Dr Peter Sloan and Dr Ross Latham for the First Steps Project.

Objective: To edit first draft.

Teacher and students revise and edit writing for publication. In this session the aim is to eliminate repetition and to use more formal, objective language.

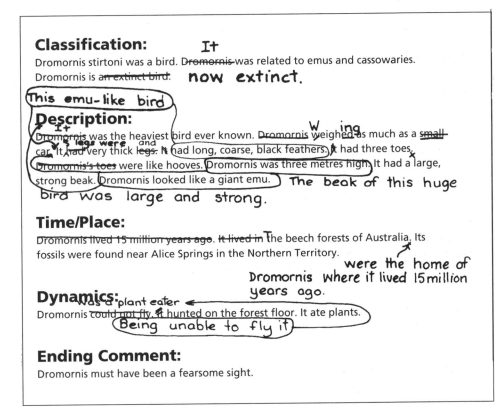

Classification: It

Dromornis stirtoni was a bird. ~~Dromornis~~ was related to emus and cassowaries. Dromornis is ~~an extinct bird.~~ now extinct.

This emu-like bird

Description:

It

Dromornis was the heaviest bird ever known. ~~Dromornis~~ weighed as much as a ~~small~~ car. It had very thick legs. It had long, coarse, black feathers. It had three toes. ~~Dromornis's toes~~ were like hooves. Dromornis was three metres high. It had a large, strong beak. Dromornis looked like a giant emu. The beak of this huge bird was large and strong.

Time/Place:

~~Dromornis lived 15 million years ago.~~ ~~It lived in~~ The beech forests of Australia. Its fossils were found near Alice Springs in the Northern Territory.

were the home of Dromornis where it lived 15 million years ago.

Dynamics: was a plant eater

Dromornis ~~could not fly.~~ It hunted on the forest floor. It ate plants.

Being unable to fly it

Ending Comment:

Dromornis must have been a fearsome sight.

Objective: To produce final report for publication.

DROMORNIS - EDITED VERSION

Dromornis Stirtoni was a bird. It was related to emus and cassowaries. Dromornis is now extinct.

Dromornis looked like a giant emu. It was the heaviest bird ever known weighing as much as a car. Dromornis was three metres high. This emu-like bird had long, coarse, black feathers. Its legs were very thick and it had only three toes which were like hooves. The beak of this bird was large and strong.

The beech forests of Australia were the home of Dromornis where it lived 15 million years ago. Its fossils were found near Alice Springs in the Northern Territory.

Dromornis was a plant-eater. Being unable to fly, it hunted on the forest floor.

Dromornis must have been a fearsome sight.

Written by Dr Peter Sloan and Dr Ross Latham for the First Steps Project.

Direct Model

Use overhead projector to display a short report (such as The Honey Bee on page 88).

Teacher asks questions of each paragraph. Students work together to build up a framework heading and understanding of the content. e.g.

Paragraph 1
What is the purpose?   To tell what it is. To introduce the subject .
What can we call it?
Classification

Paragraph 2
What is the purpose?   To tell what it looks like.
What could we call it?
Description of physical appearance

Paragraph 3
What is the purpose?   To tell where it lives
What could we call it?
Description of location

Paragraph 4
What is the purpose?   To tell what it does.
What could we call it?
Description of dynamics

Paragraph 5
What is the purpose?   To finish off the report..
What could we call it?
Summarising comment

Chart the features and the guiding questions so that children can use the framework to jointly construct a text about an animal they know. This can then be followed by research into an animal with which they are less familiar using the headings to direct their research.

Exploring Reports—a problem-solving approach

A problem solving approach is an effective way to help writers improve their report writing.

The 'Frog' texts on pages 95–6 may be used as a starting point for children to discuss reports (if they are going to write about an animal) because the framework they devise can be used, or adapted, for writing about any animal.

Share samples 1 to 4 explaining that these are samples from children about their age, and talk with students to decide which they think is the best report and why.

Children can then help to construct a reference chart with information for writing their reports about animals.

The use of planning sheets can help children with their research as headings can act as a guide.

Frogs

I reckon frogs are good.

They have big bulging eyes and they jump.

Frogs are covered with wet skin or they die.

Frogs live in trees or in water or in burrows.

frogs croak. The male ones croak really loud but the females don't.

They can be big or little.

The end.

by Anna

SAMPLE 1

Frogs

I reckon frogs are good.

They have big bulging eyes and they jump.

Frogs are covered with wet skin or they die.

Frogs live in trees or in water or in burrows.

Frogs croak. The male ones croak really loud but the females don't.

They can be big or little.

The end.

By Anna

FROGS   by Peter J.

Frogs are slippery and slimy. They can jump a long way. They croak They have wet skin. They hide sometimes. Their eyes are very big and I no some poepel who are scerd of them. I am not sceved of them. I think they are vere cute That's what I think!!!

SAMPLE 2

Frogs by Peter J.

Frogs are slippery and slimy. They can jump a long way. They croak. They have wet skin. They hide sometimes. Their eyes are very big and I know some people who are scared of them. I am not scared of them. I think they are very cute. That's what I think!!!

The frog is a small amphibious animal. Amphibians spend part of their life on land and part as a land animal.

Frogs have large back legs ~~and~~ short front legs and a flattish body with no neck. Most frogs have a sticky tongue that is attached to the frunt of the mouth. When they want food (like insects) they can flip the tongue out.

Frogs have thin wet skin with no hair. Some frogs ~~can~~ change colour and can be camouflaged from their enemies.

Frogs lay eggs, in jelly and these hatch into ~~tapo~~ tadpoles. Tadpoles change gradually into frogs. This is called metamorphosis.

Frogs are useful to humans because frogs eat insects.

Franzo L. Frogs

Frogs are animals. They live in water. They eat insects. They can be small (1 centimete) or big (30 centimetres). Frogs and toads are different. Frogs are in a lot of magic stories.

Frogs can jump a long way.

Frogs can lay eggs and these eggs can float in the water and then they can turn into tadpoles and they get legs and then they are frogs.

Frogs have to keep their skin wet or they die. Some people eat frogs legs but I wouldn't.

What I like about frogs is their eyes. They are big and round and sticky-out. Frogs and toads are a bit the same and a bit different. Frogs are good because they eat insects. Toads have warts. The only toads in Australia are cane toads.

SAMPLE 3

Tina J.

Frogs

The frog is a small amphibious animal. Amphibians spend part of their life on land and part as a land animal.

Frogs have large back legs, short front legs and a flattish body with no neck. Most frogs have a sticky tongue that is attached to the front of the mouth. When they want food, (like insects) they can flip the tongue out.

Frogs have thin wet skin with no hair. Some frogs change colour and can be camouflaged from their enemies.

Frogs lay eggs, in jelly, and these hatch into tadpoles. Tadpoles change gradually into frogs. This is called metamorphosis.

Frogs are useful to humans because frogs eat insects.

SAMPLE 4

Franzo L

Frogs

Frogs are animals. They live in water. They eat insects. They can be small (1 centimetre) or big (30 centimetres). Frogs and toads are different. Frogs are in a lot of magic stories.

Frogs can jump a long way.

Frogs can lay eggs and these eggs can float in the water and then they can turn into tadpoles and they get legs and then they are frogs.

Frogs have to keep their skin wet or they die. Some people eat frogs legs but I wouldn't.

What I like about frogs is their eyes. They are big and round and sticky-out.

Frogs and toads are a bit the same and a bit different. Frogs are good because they eat insects. Toads have warts. The only toads in Australia are Cane Toads.

Planning in Classroom Contexts

'Jigsaws'

The following is an effective way of gathering, organising and presenting information using cooperative group work. It enables children to work in heterogeneous groups and to take responsibility for their own learning. In this Social Studies topic children were investigating the effects of animals that had been imported to Australia.

Objective: to activate background knowledge of a topic

To begin a new topic whole class participated in brainstorm to activate and share current knowledge. Teacher acted as recorder, writing each suggestion on a separate card or post-it sticker.

Objective: to classify and organise information

The teacher worked with children to move cards and cluster information. Children then formed home groups and tried to decide on suitable headings for each cluster. Whole class decided which headings seem to be most appropriate.

The children decided on these headings:

Name of animal
Country of origin
Reason for importing
Effects
Eradication
Other interesting information

Objective: to jointly construct a report as a model. (Children had previously analysed and read reports.)

The teacher chose to write about Cane Toads as he had some prior knowledge of the topic. Suggestions from the children were welcomed. The teacher included the following teaching points:

- in the opening paragraph he used 'relational' verbs like *is*, *has*, *belongs to*, *classified as* to help children understand how to define and classify
- he demonstrated ways of overcoming the tendency to begin every sentence with the subject-noun (Frogs) by the careful use of pronouns, such as *it* or *they* and use of 'pointing' words e.g. *these animals, this amphibian*
- he used timeless present tense *live, inhabit, change*
- he showed how each new paragraph began with a topic sentence that introduced the information to follow
- he used precise descriptive language or scientific language. (Adverbs and adjectives are used sparingly and accurately in the language of reports.)
- he suggested children include and label diagrams or drawings to illustrate the importance of these in providing accurate information for the reader
- in the final paragraph (conclusion) he briefly repeated some important information to sum up the report
  The report was left for reference and used later to demonstrate editing techniques.

Objective: to encourage children to survey and question so that they set their own questions to be answered

Children examined the information and wrote questions to which they wanted answers. Each question was written on a separate strip of paper and left on display. These questions could be answered by anyone in the course of their research or could provide a focus for study for a particular child.

Objective: to enable children to plan and organise their writing

From a suggested list of animals each child in the home group chose a different animal to study. The headings suggested during the brainstorm provided a focus for study of each animal. Children studying the same animal formed new 'expert' groups.

Objective: to allow children to clarify the task—establishing the purpose and audience

Children were asked to collect information (using the headings from the original brainstorm as guidelines for research) and present it as a written report. They were to present their report to their original or home group. They would be the only expert, studying their chosen animal, in that group so it was essential that they did their research conscientiously. Information was to be presented in a particular format.

Children suggested turning the headings into study questions:

What is it?
Where was it from?
Why was it imported ?
What effects has it had?
What are the plans for eradication?
What else have you found?

Objective: to enable children to engage in collaborative research

Children worked in the 'expert' groups to research and collate information about their chosen topic. The emphasis was on collaboration so that each member succeeded in becoming an expert on the topic.

Children in the class brought in resources and shared their expertise. They wrote information and then revised it together. They constantly checked with each other to make sure everyone was able to proceed.

Objective: to enable children to report to an audience

Children returned to their home group and each 'expert' presented own report. Group members were encouraged to ask questions to clarify their understanding. Home group members were keen to ask questions and to supply answers.

Objective: to enable children to reflect on the knowledge they have gained

Whole class returned to the record of the original group brainstorm to compare their current understandings with previous knowledge. They referred to the questions they had wanted answered.

Objective: to enable children to reflect on group processes

Children discussed the group processes they had used and suggested any changes for the future.

Children reflected that they were surprised how much they knew and how good it felt not having to work on your own. One child who had some learning difficulties said confidently,' I like being an expert and it isn't that hard when you all work together!' Many children expressed satisfaction that they had learned a lot without any adult help.

The process described above took place over some weeks. The teacher was able to help small groups and individual children focus on their particular needs in writing and spelling. The children became very interested in the scientific names used and some started their own lists of 'Latin Words'. A great deal of reading and talking went on as children shared the limited resources. The children also seemed committed to the task as they were going to be the only expert on their topic in their group and so they felt quite responsible.

Independent Research Projects

Teachers often ask their students to conduct research into different topics. Independent research projects provide a most effective vehicle for learning how to collect and organise information while providing meaningful on-task practice in using a range of writing and reading strategies and conventions.

Independent research projects can be undertaken where children use their knowledge of the framework for their own reports.

The following plan was devised by students and teacher to help guide children in their first independent research task. There were elements of free choice, in that students could choose any imported animal to study and any way to present their Report for the audience.

Collaborative learning and resource sharing was encouraged.

Parents were invited to help in gathering resources but the 'Notes for Parents' section was emphasised. The teacher was interested in seeing the processes used by students so asked to see notebooks at various intervals. Students were able to ask the teacher for conferences whenever they needed to discuss their progress. Large chunks of time were allocated in school to enable most of the work to be completed by most children at school.

Instructions for Writing a Report

This is a copy of the instructions given to the Year 4 class.

1 **Read** about imported animals.
2 **Choose** which animal you will write about.
3 **Write** your plan. Include any information you already have. Write any questions you want to answer. **Choose** which paragraphs you will write. For example:
   What is it? Write a title
   Introduction one or more sentences telling things such as what it is, and other general information that would give the reader some idea of what you are writing about
   Physical characteristics what it looks like
   Where is it from?
   When and why was it imported?
   What effects has it had?
   What are the plans for eradication?
   What else have you found?

Conclusion a paragraph that provides an ending for your project (You might want to briefly repeat some of the most important information.)

Remember you don't have to use this plan; you can make up a different one. You can add to or delete from your plan at any time

4 Stop! Show me your notebook.

5 Take notes in your notebook like this (remember to write your short notes while looking at the text and then turn the book over and write your long notes, in your own words, without referring to the text):

Short Notes	**Long Notes**
Use key words and phrases with the reference book open.	Write your own notes reference book closed.
Cane toad	*Cane toads are the only true toads in Australia.*
Hawaii/Sth Cent America	*Australia's cane toads came from Hawaii although they are native to South and Central America.*

6 Stop! Show me your notes.

7 Now **decide** how you are going to present your research. Here are some ideas:

- chart with illustrations and notes
- tape recording with illustrations
- picture book with explanation
- comparison of two or more kinds of dinosaurs
- any other ideas you like, provided you discuss it with me first

- diorama with labels
- model with notes
- booklet

8 Put it all together. Remember that you **must** have:

- cover page
- title page with title, author
- contents page, illustration (unless you have a model)
- list of reference books. Write your list like this:
  Jones, C.D. (1981) **Native Animals of Australia** Macmillan
  Smith, A.B. (1984) **Feral Animals in Australia** Longman Cheshire
  You **might** want to have:
  - Chapters
  - index
  - copyright symbol and publisher's logo
  - glossary
  - diagrams

The following is an example of a note that may be used to inform parents about the project.

Notes for Parents

This report may seem like an enormous task but the children have done several reports in class already, although not necessarily individually and not on this topic. We have gone through the instructions in class.

The only help that your child might need is:

1 further explanation of the instructions
2 finding an appropriate reference in an encyclopaedia
3 translation of difficult text into simple language (Do this orally. Don't write it.)
4 explanation of terms.

You don't have to do any of the project. Your child should be able to do it alone. If you feel tempted to do things like help with an illustration, or tell your child what to write, or put a book together, ask yourself 'Will this help my child to learn?'

The process of doing the research and collating it is more important than the finished product, although pride in the standard of work is to be encouraged. Neatness in the published work is important. Deadlines for each stage of the project will be written in the notebook.

Planning Frameworks

The use of planning frameworks (see pages 102–5) for report writing can help children as they collect information. The framework headings provide guidance for their research.

REPORT PLAN

Purpose: to provide scientific or factual information
TOPIC:

ILLUSTRATION

CLASSIFICATION: It is an animal / insect / plant / object / person / _____ .

DESCRIPTION: It is small / medium-sized / large / as big as a _____ .

Its colour is _____

It is furry / smooth / rough / scaly / soft / slimy / _____ .

It has legs / wings / _____ .

It has _____ arms / _____ .

The _____ is _____

REPORT PLAN

Title:	
HEADINGS	**KEY WORDS - SHORT NOTES**
Classification • **What is it?**	
Description • **What attributes does it have?** **(size, shape, features)**	
Place/Time • **Where is it?** • **When is it?**	
Dynamics • **What does it do?**	
Summarising Comment	

REPORT PLAN

NAME:

INTRODUCTION TOPIC:

DESCRIPTION:

_____

Subheading

_____

_____

_____

_____

_____

_____

_____

Subheading

_____

_____

_____

_____

_____

_____

_____

Subheading

_____

_____

_____

_____

_____

CONCLUSION OR SUMMARY: A comment to sum up main points

Assessment and Evaluation of Report Writing

The continuum of indicators on the following page traces the development of Report writing. Teachers may wish to use the indicators to assess children's control of Report writing.

Samples of the combined use of the *Writing: Developmental Continuum* and the continuum for Report writing are included on pages 108–9 to show how teachers use a combination of both to evaluate children's writing. It is suggested that samples of work be examined and indicators highlighted. This information provides a basis for teaching and enables teachers to help children see how their writing can be improved.

A checklist for Reports is provided on page 110. This is made up of the indicators for the Extending stage of Report writing and can be used as a quick way of assessing children's progress in the writing of Reports.

REPORT INDICATORS

BEGINNING

Purpose:

The writer:
- discusses the purpose of written reports

Text Organisation and Content
- writes observation and comment or a recount

Classification
- sometimes attempts to generalise and classify information

Description
- focuses on a specific part of a whole class of things, e.g. 'My cat eats meat' not 'Cats eat meat.'
- includes features that are not necessarily important or relevant

Conclusion
- writes a concluding statement that is a comment rather than a summary of the report

Language Features
- uses personal or subjective language, e.g. 'I really like...'
- writes a simple description with few refined adjectives, e.g. *big, little*
- uses simple conjunctions such as *and*
- has difficulty maintaining simple present tense
- shows little evidence of writing in the third person
- writes statements about the 'here and now,' e.g. 'My cat like to chase birds.'

DEVELOPING

Purpose:

The writer:
- discusses the purpose of written reports

Text Organisation and Content
- uses part of the report framework
- introduces the topic
- writes a classification that lacks precision
- attempts to generalise
- uses some generic terms, e.g. *people, animals*

Classification
- attempts a classification or generalisation

Description
- gives limited general information in description
- is beginning to organise aspects of topics into paragraphs
- selects some important aspects to elaborate
- describes some specific features
- attempts to classify information gathered

Conclusion
- uses a simple concluding statement with some attempt to summarise what has been written

Language Features
- is beginning to use written language structures e.g. 'Pollution has invaded...'
- uses some technical or subject specific vocabulary
- uses simple conjunctions, such as *and, so, because*
- is beginning to use linking verbs, such as *is, a, has a, belongs to*
- is beginning to use timeless verbs, e.g. *fight, climb*
- is beginning to use timeless present tense
- is beginning to maintain third person

CONSOLIDATING

Purpose:

The writer:
- demonstrates understanding that reports are written to provide information

Text Organisation and Content
- uses report framework

Classification
- writes an introduction with a generalisation and/or classification

Description
- includes some accurate, detailed description of the subject, e.g. size, colour, other features
- is able to select and elaborate special features
- includes detail that is clearly related to the topic
- attempts to make comparisons that help the reader visualise aspects of the subject, e.g. 'It looked like an enormous lizard.'
- classifies information effectively for use

Conclusion
- writes a summary or concluding paragraph that includes main features of the report, e.g. 'This invention will change the course of history.'

Language Features
- organises aspects of topics into paragraphs
- uses precise subject specific vocabulary
- uses linking verbs effectively
- uses timeless action verbs effectively, e.g. *suckle, teach, fight, climb*
- maintains timeless present tense throughout
- maintains third person stance throughout

EXTENDING

Purpose:

The writer:
- demonstrates understanding that there are different types of reports and that the structure of a report depends on the purpose for which it is written
- demonstrates understanding that reports contain information that is selected, sorted and synthesised to give the reader/writer information significant to a topic or focus of study

Text Organisation and Content
- uses report framework and adapts it to suit purpose and audience

Classification
- writes an introduction that successfully classifies and/or generalises information essential to the subject of the report
- uses accurate definitions

Descriptions
- includes detailed information selected because of its relevance to the subject of the report
- elaborates on and interprets important information
- organises like information into paragraphs that link cohesively in logical order

Conclusion
- writes a conclusion that accurately identifies the main points

Language Features
- writes using a formal and objective style
- demonstrates consistent use of tense (usually timeless present tense), e.g. *are, hunt, fly, live, suckle*
- demonstrates consistent use of singular or plural generic participants, e.g. *humanity faces increasing.... the family is...*
- uses generic terms successfully, e.g. *humankind, mammals, pollutants*
- uses a range of precise subject-specific terms in context
- uses precise descriptive language
- uses linking verbs, e.g. *has a, is a, belongs to*
- uses appropriate language to compare, contrast, define or classify, e.g. *identical, related, kindred*

Sample of Report writing:

> ### REPORT
> ### Red Crabs
>
> This report is about red crabs. The red is red and black. It has two knippers and it has three back legs. I think it is 25cm long or more. They have small eyes and mouths.
>
> The red crab lives in the jungles on Christmas Island. Sometimes it lives on cliffs.
>
> The red crab cleans up Christmas Island.
>
> The red crab eats rotten mangoes and dead squashed red crabs. It grows from five centimetres to thirty

Early Writing Phase Indicators from Writing: Developmental Continuum highlighted:

The writer:
- ◆ **uses a small range of familiar text forms**
- ◆ **chooses topics that are personally significant**
- • is beginning to use some informational text structures
- • writes simple factual accounts with little elaboration
- ◆ **uses basic sentence structures and varies sentence beginnings**
- • joins simple sentences (often overusing the same connectors, e.g. 'and', 'then'
- ◆ **can explain in context, some of the purposes of using writing, e.g. shopping list or telephone messages as a memory aid**
- ◆ **experiments with words drawn from language experience activities, literature, media and oral language of peers and others**
- ◆ **begins to develop editing skills**
- ◆ **attempts to use some punctuation**
- • uses capital letters for names
- • usually maintains consistent tense
- • writes title which reflects content
- • perseveres to complete writing tasks
- ◆ **talks with others to plan and revise own writing**

Report Continuum Indicators (Developing) highlighted:

The writer:
- • discusses the purpose of written reports
- • uses part of the report framework
- • introduces the topic
- • writes a classification that lacks precision
- • gives limited general information in description
- • is beginning to organise aspects of topics into paragraphs
- • selects some important aspects to elaborate
- • describes some specific features
- • is beginning to use written language structures
- • is beginning to use timeless present tense
- • is beginning to maintain third person

This page provides an example of the combined use of the *Writing: Developmental Continuum* and the continuum for Report writing, to evaluate a sample of writing. It confirms placement on the *Writing: Developmental Continuum* and can be used to assess control of Report writing.

Sample of Report writing:

> ### Frogs
>
> The frog is a small amphibious animal. Amphibians spend part of their life on land and part as a land animalf.
>
> Frogs have large back legs ~~and~~ short front legs and a flattish body with no neck. Most frogs have a sticky tongue that is attached to the frunt of the mouth. When they want food (like insects) they can flip the tongue out.
>
> Frogs have thin wet skin with no hair. Some frogs ~~can~~ change colour and can be camouflaged from their enemies.
>
> Frogs lay eggs in jelly and these hatch into ~~tapo~~ tadpoles. Tadpoles change gradually into frogs. This is called metamorphosis.
>
> Frogs are useful to humans becase frogs eat insects.

Conventional Writing Phase Indicators from Writing: Developmental Continuum highlighted:

The writer:

- ◆ **uses text forms to suit purpose and audience**
- ◆ **can explain why some text form may be more appropriate than another to achieve a specific purpose**
- ◆ **writes a range of texts forms including stories, reports, procedures and expositions**
- • demonstrates the ability to develop a topic
- • demonstrates knowledge of differences between narrative and informational text when writing
- ◆ **uses a variety of simple, compound and extended sentences**
- ◆ **groups sentences containing related information into paragraphs**
- ◆ **is beginning to select vocabulary according to the demands of audience and purpose, e.g. uses subject-specific vocabulary**
- • edits and proof reads own writing after composing
- ◆ **uses proof-reading guide or checklist to edit own or peers' writing**
- • reorders text to clarify meaning, e.g. moves words, phrases and clauses
- ◆ **punctuates simple sentences correctly**
- • uses capital letters for proper nouns
- • uses capital letters to start sentences
- • uses capital letters for titles
- • uses full stops to end sentences
- • uses appropriate subject-verb agreements
- • uses appropriate noun-pronoun agreements
- • maintains appropriate tense throughout text
- ◆ **uses a range of strategies for planning, revising and publishing own written texts**
- • selects relevant information from a variety of sources before writing
- • can transfer information from reading to writing, e.g. takes notes for project
- • attempts to organise ideas before writing
- • uses knowledge of other texts as models for writing

Report Continuum Indicators (Consolidating) highlighted:

The writer:

- • demonstrates understanding that reports are written to provide information
- • uses report framework
- • writes an introduction with a generalisation and or classification
- • includes some accurate, detailed description of the subject, e.g. size, colour, other features
- • is able to select and elaborate special features
- • includes detail that is clearly related to the topic
- • classifies information effectively for use
- • writes a summary or concluding paragraph that includes main features of the report, e.g. 'This invention will change the course of history.'
- • organises aspects of topics into paragraphs
- • uses precise subject specific vocabulary
- • maintains timeless present tense throughout
- • maintains third person stance throughout

This page provides an example of the combined use of the *Writing: Developmental Continuum* and the continuum for Report writing, to evaluate a sample of writing. It confirms placement on the *Writing: Developmental Continuum* and can be used to assess control of Report writing.

CHECKLIST FOR REPORTS	ALWAYS	SOMETIMES	NOT YET

Purpose:

The writer:
- demonstrates understanding that there are different types of reports and that the structure of a report depends on the purpose for which it is written
- demonstrates understanding that reports contain information that is selected, sorted and synthesised to give the reader/writer information significant to a topic or focus of study

Text Organisation and Content
- uses report framework and adapts it to suit purpose and audience

Classification
- writes an introduction that successfully classifies and/or generalises information essential to the subject of the report
- uses accurate definitions

Descriptions
- includes detailed information selected because of its relevance to the subject of the report
- elaborates on and interprets important information
- organises like information into paragraphs that link cohesively in logical order

Conclusion
- writes a conclusion that accurately identifies the main points

Language Features
- writes using a formal and objective style
- demonstrates consistent use of tense (usually timeless present tense), e.g. are, *hunt, fly, live, suckle*
- demonstrates consistent use of singular or plural generic participants, e.g. *humanity faces increasing...*, *the family is...*
- uses generic terms successfully, e.g. *humankind, mammals, pollutants*
- uses a range of precise subject-specific terms in context
- uses precise descriptive language
- uses linking verbs, e.g. *has a, is a, belongs to*
- uses appropriate language to compare, contrast, define or classify, e.g. *identical, related, kindred*

Chapter 7:

Explanations

An explanation is an oral or written text that seeks to explain how things come to be the way they are, or to analyse how things work.

Features of Explanations

Purpose
The purpose of an explanation is to give an account of some phenomenon

Focus
General processes and non-human participants, e.g. erosion, electricity

Types
Explanations seem to fall into two main types:
Those that explain how things are, e.g. How a Kite Works.
Those that explain why things are, e.g. Why Volcanoes Erupt.
Some explanations may combine how and why.

Examples
Explanations may be in the form of essays, handbooks, science, health and social studies texts.

Health	Explain the process of digestion.
Social Studies	Explain why soil erosion occurs.
Science	Explain how electricity is generated.

Text Organisation
Each part of the explanation framework is at least one separate paragraph.

Explanations generally begin with a **Definition** or **Statement** about the phenomena. The definition may or may not be a classifying statement. It is often in the form of a heading or question, e.g. How is rain formed?

A description of **Components** or **Parts** generally follows.

The next stage is a logical description of the **Operation** which outlines how or why it works.

There may also be a description of the **Application** that tells when and where it works or is applied.

Some explanations also include information about **Special Features** or an **Evaluative Summary**.

Language Features

- Generalised non-human participants (the wind, glaciers, computers)
- Time relationships (first, then, following, finally)
- Cause-and-effect relationships (if/then, so, as a consequence, since)
- Mainly action verbs (material processes); (falls, rises, changes)
- Some passives (is saturated, are changed)
- Timeless present tense (are, happens, turns)

(Adapted from Derewianka B. 1990, *Exploring How Texts Work*, p. 62.)

EXPLANATION

How a Kite Works

A kite is a flying object that is heavier than air.

A kite consists of a frame, a skin covering the frame and a long string that is held by the user.

A kite becomes airborne when the wind pressure between the kite and the ground lifts the structure into the air. The tilt of the plane surface of the kite causes a lesser air pressure to occur behind the kite's upper surface than the wind on the under-surface.

Kites have been used as signals, experimental instruments in atmospheric measurement and as play objects dating back many thousands of years.

EXPLANATION

- **Definition of Phenomenon**
  - What is being explained.
- **Sequenced Explanation**

Components / Parts
  - Description of the parts.

Operations
  - How it works...
  - Why it works...
  - Cause and effect.

Applications
  - When and where it works or is applied (where applicable).

Interesting Comments, Special Features, Evaluation (where applicable).

Explanation Framework

	How a Kite Works	
Generalised non-human participants - kites	A kite is a flying object that is heavier than air.	Definition states what the thing or process is
Timeless present tense, e.g. consists, becomes	A kite <u>consists</u> of a frame, a skin covering the frame and a long string that is held by the user.	Components or parts
Cause and effect described	A kite <u>becomes</u> airborne when the wind pressure between the kite and the ground lifts the structure into the air. The tilt of the plane surface of the kite causes a lesser air pressure to occur behind the kite's upper surface than the pressure created by the wind on the under-surface.	Operation or how it works
Some passives	Kites have been used as signals, experimental instruments in atmospheric measurement and as play objects dating back many thousands of years.	Application - where it works

Framework and text written by Dr Peter Sloan and Dr Ross Latham for the First Steps Project.

How a Kite Works

A kite is a flying object that is heavier than air.

A kite consists of a frame, a skin covering the frame and a long string that is held by the user.

A kite becomes airborne when the wind pressure between the kite and the ground lifts the structure into the air. The tilt of the plane surface of the kite causes a lesser air pressure to occur behind the kite's upper surface than the pressure created by the wind on the under-surface.

Kites have been used as signals, experimental instruments in atmospheric measurement and as play objects dating back many thousands of years.

This simple text uses a recognisable Explanation framework and may be used by teachers to analyse the features of an Explanation. See activities on page 116.

Written by Dr Peter Sloan and Dr Ross Latham for the First Steps Project.

Exploring and Planning Explanations

For children in Role play, Experimental and Early Phases of writing development it is necessary to give many opportunities to practise oral explanations that focus on cause and effect.

Children operating in the Conventional or Proficient Phase of writing need to write explanations in many different contexts and, because it is a form that seems quite difficult to write effectively, it is important that they be very familiar with the subject matter before being asked to write about it. The following activities are suitable to help children understand explanations.

Informal explanations

Planning oral explanations

Shared reading

Tell your partner

Tell from the diagram

Direct model

Modelled writing

Joint construction

Sentence combining

Independent construction

Activities

Informal Explanations

When talking to children encourage them to reflect on things that are happening around them so that they begin to think about causes and effects, e.g.

How does your invention work?
Why did the block building fall down?
Why did your boat float?
How can you design a boat that floats?
How does a car engine work?
Why didn't the wolf eat the third little pig?

Planning Oral Explanations

Very young children share spontaneously and their language skills often focus on labelling and describing attributes rather than explaining how things occur, e.g. I made this truck and it's red. It's made of boxes. Teachers can extend that language by providing a framework to guide children to reflect on the processes involved in making things, e.g.

What is it called?
What did you need to make it?
How did you make it?
How does it work? Why does it work?
Did you have any problems? What did you do?

By using this framework as a guide to questioning and facilitation or as an explicit framework to be followed by children as they share something they have made, teachers are helping children to use the language of explanation.

Shared Reading

Exposure to different explanatory texts will help children to internalise the language used and to understand the structure of the text.

Many companies and some government departments print brochures, posters or booklets that explain aspects of their operation. These are generally well written and have illustrations to support text. Some that have been used successfully to support topics in the classroom include material from Australia Post, Telecom, Conservation and Land Management Authority, Agricultural Department, a brick manufacturer, an oil and gas producer, a mining company, a conservation council, health department and various trade magazines. Teachers may find it helpful to build a collection of these for references.

Look for and list cause and effect signal words

When students are reading, frame questions to help them make connections between cause and effect. Encourage children to find signal words that indicate cause and effect. As words are found, display them so that they can be used in students' writing.

Words to look for might include: if… then, becomes… when, causes, effects, in view of, because so, as a result, since, as, consequently, makes, results in, creates, forms, therefore, for this reason, hence, due to, brings about, by reason of, on account of, gives rise to, makes, produces.

Tell Your Partner

After reading a section of text ask children to explain to a partner what they have just read. Make sure they include reasons.

Tell From The Diagram

Using a text that has an explanatory diagram, ask children to work together to write an explanation of the phenomenon illustrated.

Direct Model

Use an overhead projector to display an explanation relevant to curriculum context (such as How A Kite Works page 114.) Ask questions of each paragraph. Students work together to build up a framework of headings and understanding of the content. Attach framework labels e.g.

Title	Tells the reader what phenomenon is to be explained
Definition Paragraph 1	Tells what it is
Components or parts Paragraph 2	Describes the components
Operation Paragraph 3	Tells how it works (cause and effect)
Application Paragraph 4	Tells where it can be used

Chart the features and the guiding questions so that children can use the framework to jointly construct a relevant explanation later.

Modelled Writing

Model the writing of an explanation about a familiar topic that is related to a curriculum area, e.g. How Rain is Formed. Focus on the reasons for each occurrence in the process and include a range of cause and effect linking words. Use timeless present tense, e.g. Rain is formed by… Use some passive verbs, e.g. The clouds are formed by… The process is continued …

Joint Construction

Collaborative or shared writing will help children move towards independent writing of explanations. Choose a familiar topic in the context of the curriculum and ask children to meet in small groups to brainstorm and compile information they can remember about the topic. They then categorise their information using headings from the explanation framework planning sheets on pages 122–3 and discuss any points that need to be clarified. The teacher, with help from the children, scribes the first and second paragraph. As the children are contributing ideas the teacher can explicitly discuss aspects of the construction such as the language features or text organisation necessary to achieve a clear explanation. This process may continue over a number of sessions. Alternatively, after the first session children can move back to their groups and jointly construct the remainder of the text. Groups can then share and discuss features of their explanations. The finished texts can be left for reference.

Sentence Combining

To help children write more effective and complex sentences, such as those used in explanations, try some sentence combining activities. These can be done using children's writing as a starting point, e.g.
Water evaporates into the air.
The warm air containing the water rises.
The temperature of the air drops.
The water condenses.

Could become:
Condensation occurs when warm air containing evaporated water is cooled as it rises.

By conducting these activities using children's writing teachers have the opportunity to demonstrate how writing can change from 'talk written down' to more complex and mature written language. Children are also more able to comprehend texts written in this way as they can de-construct them more easily.

Independent Construction

Use a plan
Children seem better able to organise their information if they use a written plan to record the main points of their text. (See sample on page 119.) The use of suitable headings can help guide and organise writing content.

Use diagrams
Texts such as explanations are often accompanied by diagrams, flow charts or pictures that support the written texts. Children should be encouraged to include these in their explanations.

Different Forms of Writing—a problem-solving approach

A Year Six teacher's program for Terms 2 and 3 exploring one topic with many forms of language.
Ribbons of Blue Program / Swan River / Land Use & Abuse.

Children are landowners carrying out a horticultural / farming venture on a property on the Swan River. Look at issues (environmental) concerning their farming techniques, government zoning on the land etc. Culminate in the sale of the property.

1   INTRODUCTION
Revise different forms of writing and purpose for each. Use appropriate A3 charts.

2   NARRATIVE
Write a narrative included factual information on your Avon Descent weekend i.e. comment on salt in water, colour, erosion, landscapes / property uses etc.

3   LETTER WRITING
Write to appropriate Govt Dept to obtain information about WA's Waterways, i.e. C.A.L.M., Water Authority, Agriculture Dept, R.O.B. etc.

4   PROCEDURE
Design a Govt Dept poster showing landowners on how to 'Protect the Swan River'. Incorporate R.O.B. data results—Action Plan devised according to the pH, salt results.

5   DESCRIPTION
Children complete a map of their property. Include features and special conservation features on their map. A written description of their property will be included. Revise mapping skills—scale. Include tree planting etc.

6   REPORT
Complete a report on the use and abuse of the Swan River. Present on A3. Preview characteristics of rivers in general.

7   EXPLANATION
Children write explanation as a C.A.L.M. officer explaining how erosion occurs and in particular on the upper reaches of the Swan. Include photos of 1993 and 1985 etc. to show effects of erosion.

8   EXPOSITION
Write about conflicts of interest once your property has been sold i.e. industrial developers have bought your property and will develop their factory. Write expositions from both points of view.

9   PROJECT: PLANNING
Select a form of farming that is sustainable on small acreage i.e. 10–20 acres / 4–8 ha. Look at market costs etc.

10   PROJECT: ORGANISING
Ensure all factual data is consistently presented in all the forms of writing.

11   PROJECT: WRITING
Thursday p.m.—one phase each week.

12   ADVERTISEMENT
Write an advertisement for the sale of your property. Include features, picture etc. View samples from estate agents etc.   *Year 6 Upper Swan Primary School*

EXPLANATION PLAN

Write information in each section.

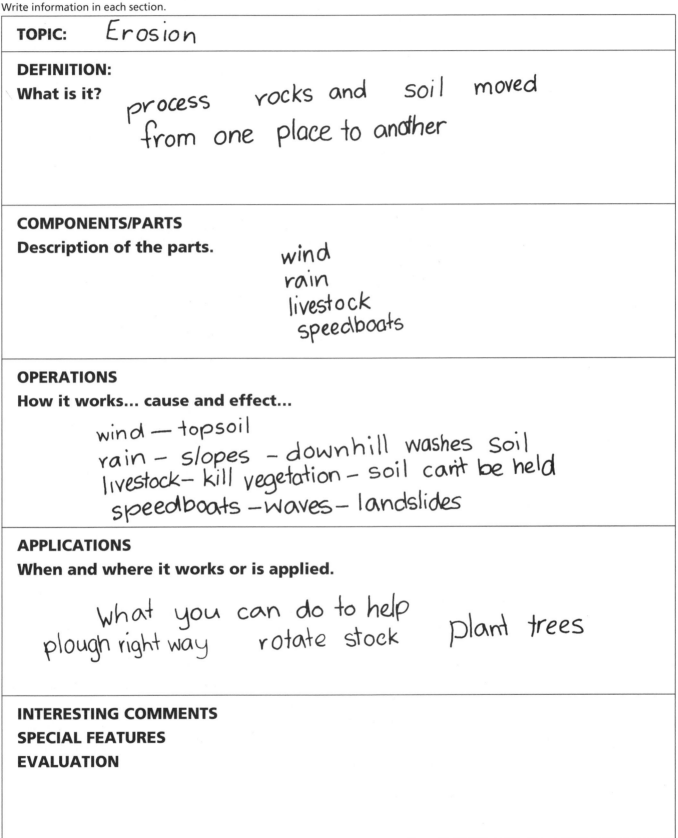

TOPIC: Erosion

DEFINITION:
What is it?

process rocks and soil moved from one place to another

COMPONENTS/PARTS
Description of the parts.

wind
rain
livestock
speedboats

OPERATIONS
How it works... cause and effect...

wind — topsoil
rain — slopes — downhill washes soil
livestock— kill vegetation — soil can't be held
speedboats —waves— landslides

APPLICATIONS
When and where it works or is applied.

What you can do to help
plough right way   rotate stock   Plant trees

INTERESTING COMMENTS
SPECIAL FEATURES
EVALUATION

HOW EROSION OCCURS

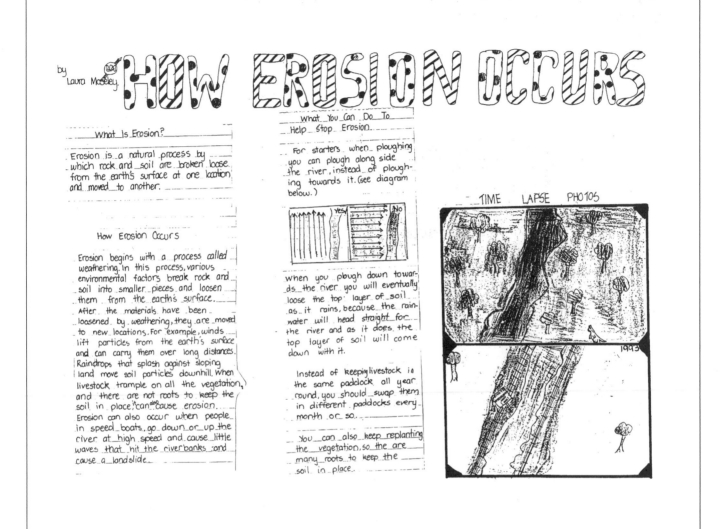

By Laura M

What Is Erosion?

Erosion is a natural process by which rock and soil are broken loose from the earth's surface at one location and moved to another.

How Erosion Occurs

Erosion begins with a process called weathering. In this process, various environmental factors break rock and soil into smaller pieces and loosen them from the earth's surface and can carry them over long distances. Raindrops that splash against sloping land move soil particles downhill. When livestock trample on all the vegetation, and there are not roots to keep the soil in place, it can also cause erosion. Erosion can also occur when people in speed boats, go down or up the river at high speed and cause little waves that hit the riverbanks and cause a landslide.

What You Can Do To Help Stop Erosion.

For starters, when ploughing you can plough along side the river, instead of ploughing towards it. (See diagram below).

When you plough down towards the river, you will eventually loose the top layer of soil as it rains, because the rainwater will head straight for the river and as it does the top layer of soil will come down with it.

Instead of keeping livestock in the same paddock all year round, you should swap them in different paddocks every month or so.

You can also keep re-plant the vegetation, so there are many roots to keep the soil in place.

Planning Frameworks

Diagrams and notes on explanation planning frameworks (see pages 122–3) will help
children to include all necessary information.

EXPLANATION PLAN

TOPIC:

DEFINITION **What is it?**	**COMPONENTS/PARTS** **Description of the parts**
OPERATIONS **How it works...**	**OPERATIONS** **cause and effect...**
APPLICATIONS	**INTERESTING COMMENTS** **SPECIAL FEATURES** **EVALUATION**

EXPLANATION PLAN

Write information in each section.

TOPIC:

DEFINITION:
What is it?

COMPONENTS/PARTS
Description of the parts.

OPERATIONS
How it works... cause and effect...

APPLICATIONS
When and where it works or is applied.

INTERESTING COMMENTS
SPECIAL FEATURES
EVALUATION

Assessment and Evaluation of Explanation Writing

The continuum of indicators on the following page traces the development of Explanation writing. Teachers may wish to use the indicators to assess children's control of Explanation writing.

Samples of the combined use of the *Writing: Developmental Continuum* and the continuum for Explanation writing are included on pages 126–7 to show how teachers use a combination of both to evaluate children's writing. It is suggested that samples of work be examined and indicators highlighted. The information provided forms a basis for teaching and enables teachers to help children see how their writing can be improved.

A checklist for Explanations is provided on page 128. This is made up of the indicators for the Extending stage of Explanation writing and can be used as a quick way of assessing children's progress in writing Explanations.

EXPLANATION INDICATORS

BEGINNING

Purpose:
The writer:
- discusses cause and effect

Text Organisation and Content
- writes observation and comment, e.g. 'Snow is made from water and it's cold.'

Phenomenon
- makes personal opening statement, e.g. 'I am going to tell how…'
- includes 'is when' in definition, e.g. 'Snow is when…'
- is unable to generalise

Sequence
- explains using subjective language, e.g. 'It makes me feel cold' instead of 'It lowers body temperature.'

Language Features
- uses common connectives, e.g. *and, then*
- includes clichés and slang, e.g. 'It goes as fast as a rocket.'

DEVELOPING

Purpose:
The writer:
- discusses some instances where written explanations are used

Text Organisation and Content
- attempts use of explanation framework

Phenomenon
- attempts generalisations but may revert to specifics

Sequence
- attempts to explain links between cause and effect, e.g. *if… then… because*

Language Features
- begins to use objective language to explain phenomena
- attempts use of passive tense, e.g. *is driven by*
- uses simple present tense, e.g. *happens, turns*
- uses some subject specific terms

CONSOLIDATING

Purpose:
The writer:
- recognises that the purpose of explanations is to explain the way things are or how things work and to give reasons for the phenomenon

Text Organisation and Content
- plans and organises information using a suggested framework

Phenomenon
- is beginning to define terms precisely using 'having', 'being', 'making' verbs
- provides a focus for the reader
- begins to generalise effectively

Sequence
- includes information in logical sequence to explain how or why a phenomenon occurs
- generally explains links between cause and effect
- uses objective language

Language Features
- uses passive voice, e.g. *saturated, is cooled by*
- uses cause and effect linking words , e.g. *if, then, when, why*
- uses simple present tense consistently
- uses a range of subject specific terms

EXTENDING

Purpose:
The writer:
- demonstrates understanding that there are different types of explanations that link cause and effect and to describe processes such as how or why something works
- uses explanations to provide reasons for the appearance of certain phenomena

Text Organisation and Content
- independently plans and organises sufficient information to enable the explanation to be easily followed

Phenomenon
- begins with a clear, precise statement of the phenomenon, e.g. 'Igneous rock is formed when molten rock cools and solidifies'

Sequence
- selects and elaborates appropriate information such as a description of components, how it works or why it works
- effectively links information to clearly demonstrate the relationship of cause and effect
- writes events in logical sequence; includes an evaluation if applicable

Language Features
- uses appropriate subject specific terms and technical vocabulary and includes definition of terms as required
- maintains cohesion through reference to generalised non human participants, e.g. rocks, seasons, land breezes, mountains, combustion, flight
- uses some passives such as *is caused, is affected, are cooled*
- uses linking word to signify cause and effect, e.g. *then, consequently, the result is*

Sample of Explanation writing:

HOW EROSION OCCURS

Erosion Occurs when there is a creek or brook and very few trees are near. So when the water comes gushing down it washes dirt, sand, clay ect there is a way to prevent this by planting trees. The trees roots are like arms in the soil which hold it together so your creek, brook won't be crumbling So start planting trees it will stop erosion and make it a better country.

Early Writing Phase Indicators from Writing: Developmental Continuum highlighted:

The writer:

- ◆ **uses a small range of familiar text forms**
- ◆ **chooses topics that are personally significant**
- • uses a partial organisational framework
- • is beginning to use some informational text structures
- • writes simple factual accounts will little elaboration
- ◆ **uses basic sentence structures and varies sentence beginnings**
- ◆ **can explain in context, some of the purposes of using writing, e.g. shopping list or telephone messages as a memory aid**
- ◆ **experiments with words drawn from language experience activities, literature, media and oral language of peers and others**
- ◆ **begins to develop editing skills**
- ◆ **attempts to use some punctuation**

Explanation Continuum Indicators (Beginning) highlighted:

The writer:

- • discusses cause and effect
- • includes 'is when' in definition, e.g. 'Snow is when…'
- • explains using subjective language, e.g. 'It makes me feel cold' instead of 'It lowers body temperature.'

This page provides an example of the combined use of the *Writing: Developmental Continuum* and the continuum for Explanation writing, to evaluate a sample of writing. It confirms placement on the *Writing: Developmental Continuum* and can be used to assess control of Explanation writing.

Sample of Explanation writing:

HOW EROSION OCCURS

The wind at the soil surface is one of the most important factors affecting erosion. Erosion of the land by wind and water has destroyed thousands of acres of good agricultural land in other countries. Wind erosion, often known as blowing, starts with a process known as saltation, which is sort of a jumping motion of the smallest, most erodible particles of soil. With successive blows the eroded soil becomes more softer as most of the fine material is blown away. Sometimes when people walk on plants they die, so there's lack of plants and soil breaks away. When the farmers have got their vineyards close to the river the ploughing can break up soil, because it would be smooth and it would cause erosion. Erosion is caused by soil wearing away. Also if the farmer has crops growing down the hill the water that runs down will make the soil break and then crops won't have any good soil to grow in, so their for what ever the farmer was doing with them he won't be able to. The two main agents of erosion are wind + soil + water. In regions of very low rainfall there can naturally be little erosion caused by rain. further, what little rain does fall, is mainly taken up by a vegetation permanently short of water so their is little run off. Erosion always has taken place, and always will. The surface of the earth is constantly changing with mountains rising, valleys being cut deeper + wider, the coast line receding here, advancing here.

Conventional Writing Phase Indicators from Writing: Developmental Continuum highlighted:

The writer:

- ◆ **uses text forms to suit purpose and audience**
- ◆ **can explain why some text form may be more appropriate than another to achieve a specific purpose**
- ◆ **writes a range of text forms including stories, reports, procedures and expositions**
- • demonstrates the ability to develop a topic
- • demonstrates knowledge of differences between narrative and informational text when writing
- ◆ **uses a variety of simple, compound and extended sentences**
- ◆ **is beginning to select vocabulary according to the demands of audience and purpose, e.g. uses subject-specific vocabulary**
- ◆ **uses proof reading guide or checklist to edit own or peers' writing**
- ◆ **punctuates simple sentences correctly**
- • uses capital letters for proper nouns
- • uses capital letters to start sentences
- • uses capital letters for titles
- • uses full stops to end sentences
- • sometimes uses commas
- • writes apostrophes for contractions
- • maintains appropriate tense throughout text
- ◆ **uses a range of strategies for planning, revising and publishing own written texts**
- • selects relevant information from a variety of sources before writing
- • can transfer information from reading to writing, e.g. takes notes for project
- • attempts to organise ideas before writing
- • plans writing using notes, lists or diagrams or other relevant information
- • uses knowledge of other texts as models for writing

Explanation Continuum Indicators (Consolidating) highlighted:

The writer:

- • recognises that the purpose of explanations is to explain the way things are and to give reasons for the phenomenon
- • plans and organises information using a suggested framework
- • is beginning to define terms precisely using 'having', 'being', 'making' verbs
- • begins to generalise effectively
- • includes information in logical sequence to explain how or why a phenomenon occurs
- • generally explains links between cause and effect
- • uses objective language
- • uses passive voice, e.g. *saturated, is cooled by*
- • uses cause and effect linking words, e.g. *if, then, when, why*
- • uses simple present tense consistently

This page provides an example of the combined use of the *Writing: Developmental Continuum* and the continuum for Explanation writing, to evaluate a sample of writing. It confirms placement on the *Writing: Developmental Continuum* and can be used to assess control of Explanation writing.

CHECKLIST FOR EXPLANATIONS	ALWAYS	SOMETIMES	NOT YET

Purpose:

The writer:
- demonstrates understanding that there are different types of explanations that link cause and effect and to describe processes such as how or why something works
- uses explanations to provide reasons for the appearance of certain phenomena

Text Organisation and Content
- independently plans and organises sufficient information to enable the explanation to be easily followed

Phenomenon
- begins with a clear, precise statement of the phenomenon, e.g. 'Igneous rock is formed when molten rock cools and solidifies'

Sequence
- selects and elaborates appropriate information such as a description of components, how it works or why it works
- effectively links information to clearly demonstrate the relationship of cause and effect
- writes events in logical sequence; includes an evaluation if applicable

Language Features
- uses appropriate subject specific terms and technical vocabulary and includes definition of terms as required
- maintains cohesion through reference to generalised non-human participants, e.g. rocks, seasons, land breezes, mountains, combustion, flight
- uses some passives such as *is caused, is affected, are cooled*
- uses linking word to signify cause and effect, e.g. *then, consequently, the result is*

Chapter 8:

Expositions

An exposition is the critical evaluation of ideas involving argument, persuasion or debate.

Features of Expositions

Purpose
The purpose of an exposition is to develop ideas and supporting details in order to present a logical argument from a particular point of view.

Focus
Logical reasoning is the main focus of expositions

Types
Expositions may be written:

- to persuade readers to agree with a writer's particular point of view or thesis
- to compare and/or contrast topics and develop a case that will persuade the reader that the writer's premise is correct
- to analyse a topic, presenting all points of view and stating the logical conclusion or expecting that the reader will form a logical conclusion (based on the information provided by the writer).

The generic structure of each type of exposition is the same.

Examples
Expositions may be in the form of essays, letters, policies, critical reviews, advertisements.

English	Does television promote crime in the community?
Health	Sponsorship in sport—is it necessary?
Social Studies	Compare modern and ancient modes of transport
Science	Electricity and magnetism are closely related

Text Organisation
Each part of the exposition framework is a separate section of the text and may include more than one paragraph. The argument section, in particular, may be lengthy if it contains a number of for and against arguments.

Expositions generally begin with a statement of the basic position to be taken and/or an overview of the topic or question. This is the *Thesis*.

This is followed by an **Assertion** or **Argument** with supporting evidence. Generally the argument 'for' is stated first and the argument 'against' is stated last. In some texts there may be more than one assertion to be examined.

The exposition ends with a **Conclusion** or **Summary** that maybe in the form of an evaluation, a restatement of the position and/or a re-defining of the argument(s).

Language Features:

- Generalised participants—sometimes human but often abstract
- Possibility of technical terms relating to the issue
- Variety of verb (process) types—action (material), linking (relational), saying (verbal) and mental
- Mainly timeless present tense when presenting position and points in the argument, but might change according to the stage of the text (e.g. if historical background to the issue is being given, the tense will obviously change to the past; if predictions are being made, the tense might change to the future)
- Frequent use of passives to help structure the text
- Actions are often changed into 'things' (nominalised) to make the argument sound more objective and to help structure the text
- Connectives associated with reasoning (therefore, so, because of, the first reason, etc.)

(Adapted from Derewianka B. 1990, *Exploring How Texts Work*, pp. 76-78.)

EXPOSITION

Car Colour and Road Safety

Many road accidents happen at night. A major reason for this is that certain colours are not easily observed in poor light conditions. Thus cars painted in those colours are not easily noticed by other drivers.

One solution, would be to legislate that all cars be painted yellow or white. This would overcome the problem of poor visibility due to car colour and thus reduce traffic accidents related to it.

Yellow and white are the two paint surfaces that reflect most light. For this reason, yellow is used as a background on road signs and other important signals. Moreover, yellow and white are not generally problems for the colour-blind.

The problem with this solution is that people have strong preference with regard to colour. They like their cars to have some distinctiveness. It is an emotional issue.

Although there may be emotional resistance to this idea of painting all cars yellow or white, the life-saving benefits must surely outweigh the conditioned colour fads of motorists.

EXPOSITION

- **Thesis**
  - What position is to be taken?
  - What background information is needed?
  - What general line will follow?
- **Assertions / Arguments**
  - What points are important to support the stated position?
  - What evidence and examples will strengthen the case?
- **Summary / Conclusion**
  - How can the points be reiterated to evaluate and concisely re-define the position taken?

Exposition Framework

CAR COLOUR AND ROAD SAFETY

General issues. Impersonal writing.	Many road accidents happen at night. A major reason for this is that certain colours are not easily observed in poor light conditions. Thus cars painted in those colours are not easily noticed by other drivers.	Thesis - overview of topic stating basic position.
Some passives, e.g. that all cars be painted.	One solution, would be to legislate that all cars be painted yellow or white. This would overcome the problem of poor visibility due to car colour and thus reduce traffic accidents related to it.	Assertion or argument for
Linking words to do with reasoning, e.g. for this reason, thus moreover, problem.	Yellow and white are the two paint surfaces that reflect most light. For this reason, yellow is used as a background on road signs and other important signals. Moreover, yellow and white are not generally problems for the colour-blind.	Evidence
	The problem with this solution is that people have strong preference with regard to colour. They like their cars to have some distinctiveness. It is an emotional issue.	Assertion or argument against.
Nominalisation - actions become things, e.g. have some distinctiveness, emotional resistance.	Although there may be emotional resistance to this idea of painting all cars yellow or white, the life-saving benefits must surely outweigh the conditioned colour fads of motorists.	Evaluation and reiteration of position taken.

Framework and text written by Dr Peter Sloan and Dr Ross Latham for the First Steps Project.

131

CAR COLOUR AND ROAD SAFETY

Many road accidents happen at night. A major reason for this is that certain colours are not easily observed in poor light conditions. Thus cars painted in those colours are not easily noticed by other drivers.

One solution, would be to legislate that all cars be painted yellow or white. This would overcome the problem of poor visibility due to car colour and thus reduce traffic accidents related to it.

Yellow and white are the two paint surfaces that reflect most light. For this reason, yellow is used as a background on road signs and other important signals. Moreover, yellow and white are not generally problems for the colour-blind.

The problem with this solution is that people have strong preference with regard to colour. They like their cars to have some distinctiveness. It is an emotional issue.

Although there may be emotional resistance to this idea of painting all cars yellow or white, the life-saving benefits must surely outweigh the conditioned colour fads of motorists.

This simple text uses a recognisable Exposition framework and may be used by teachers to introduce and analyse the features of an Exposition. See activity on page 134.

Written by Dr Peter Sloan and Dr Ross Latham for the First Steps Project.

Exploring and Planning Expositions

Take advantage of authentic experiences and real issues in which children are interested and model writing a case for or against a particular viewpoint. Issues such as the environment, school routines and rules, health issues, misleading advertising and general social issues can be addressed through writing letters to relevant authorities, or media outlets. Advertisements and posters can be prepared to put a case and so on. Children will see how powerful and useful this form of writing is when they see results.

Activities

Many areas of the curriculum provide topics for discussion where both sides of an argument are examined. The ability to build a case and present it, including relevant information, will rely largely on the student's ability to initiate and sustain a discussion and to amass suitable evidence. These skills are probably best practised in partner and small group discussions about relevant and familiar topics.

When students have had many oral opportunities to shape their assertions and evidence into a logical and cohesive argument they are better equipped to engage in written expositions.

The following suggestions for activities will help develop understandings of the features of written expositions.

Informal and formal debates

Be the expert

Change the point of view

Character defences

Examining persuasive tactics

Direct model

Modelled and shared writing

Problem-solving approach

Informal and Formal Debates

Take advantage of relevant current topics to provide authentic reasons for debates. Encourage students to gather their information and organise it before presenting their assertions. After the debate ask students to reflect on the features that made one person's case more convincing than another.

Be The Expert

Start with a topic that is of interest to students, e.g. Children should do homework every day. Decide who would have a vested interest in the topic, e.g. students, parents, teachers, sports coaches, TV channels. Allocate these roles to students so that there is an equal number of each stakeholder. Students work in groups (all the teachers together, all the parents etc.) to discuss the statement from their role's point of view and make notes to help them remember the main points. They will become the experts in their role. Students then re-form groups so that each group has one of each stakeholder. Group members take turns to present the case from his/her stakeholder's point of view. Questions may be asked after everyone has presented a case.

Change the Point of View

After reading a story ask children to retell it from a different point of view, e.g. the wolf in Red Riding Hood.

Character Defences

After reading a story children form groups to prepare a case to decide why they should be retained in the book, e.g. different groups would take the roles of the wolf, grandmother, woodcutter etc.

Examining Persuasive Tactics

Ask children to collect advertisements and group them into categories, e.g. food advertisements, make-up ads, car ads etc. Students take one category per group and decide how advertisements persuade people to buy products. Suggest they look for information that is stated and that which is implied.

Direct Model

Use overhead projector to display an exposition relevant to curriculum context (such as Car Colour and Road Safety from page 132).

Ask questions about each paragraph. Students work together to build up framework headings and understanding of the content of each section. Attach framework labels, e.g.

Title	Gives the reader a broad idea of the topic
Paragraph 1 *Thesis*	States problem and point of view to be developed
Paragraph 2 *Argument and evidence for*	Gives first argument and evidence
Paragraph 3 *Argument and evidence for*	Gives next argument and evidence
Paragraph 4 *Argument and evidence against*	Gives counter argument
Paragraph 5 *Conclusion*	Gives a concise summary and reiterates arguments

Chart the features and the guiding questions so that children can use the framework to jointly construct a relevant expository text.

Modelled and Shared Writing

Points to remember when conducting modelled writing or shared writing sessions for expositions.

- provide opportunities for children to share their opinions and ideas about the topic
- stress the need to present the facts without distortion
- stress the need to gather evidence to support an argument. It is not enough to list the assertions without evidence or data to support them

- stress the need to have a definite point of view on an issue before attempting to write a persuasive text
- talk about the way you present a case by appealing to emotions while sounding very detached and objective
- demonstrate how to organise arguments logically
- demonstrate how to present both sides of a case as well as one side
- use passive tense to help structure the text (the delicate ecological balance has been upset by horses, rather than horses upset the ecological balance)
- talk about the use of precise vocabulary appropriate to the topic
- demonstrate the use of words to use instead of slang or words that may be more appropriate to oral language
- talk about the use of topic sentences and supporting details grouped into paragraphs
- talk about the differences between 'talk written down' and written language

Exploring Expositions—a problem-solving approach

Year 7 students were studying a unit entitled Co-operation and Conflict when they read, in the local newspaper, a controversial article about horses and riders being allowed access to a nearby National Park. They decided to join the debate by writing to the editor to put forward their viewpoints. They had a clear purpose and audience for writing. The teacher decided not to give any instructions about writing, although children were encouraged to read other letters to the editor before they began. The teacher privately asked four children's permission to type their letters for class analysis (omitting names). Children had analysed texts previously and understood the process.

The samples on page 136 were the texts used to help children ascertain which was the most successful text and why.

HORSES IN JOHN FORREST NATIONAL PARK

SAMPLE 1

I reckon they should be banned because they eat the trees and grass.

Horses are domestic animals and the parks should be left for native animals like kangaroos and that.

Near our house there is a paddock with horses in it and they have eaten all the grass and killed the trees. Some people like to have horses so that's okay but they shouldn't expect to let them go eating all our parks.

SAMPLE 2

Horses should be banned from John Forrest National Park because our native fauna and flora are being threatened. The delicate ecological balance has already been upset because horses have eaten native plants and spread noxious weeds.

Horse owners show little regard for our parks as they often let their horses stray from designated bridle paths. Evidence of this can be seen when bush walking as there is disgusting, smelly horse manure on the footpaths. Oats, barley and other grass seeds are carried in manure and soon germinate. Introduced grasses have already taken over in many areas. If horse owners are irresponsible, horses must be excluded from the area.

Horses ring bark trees. Trees provide much needed shelter and food for many animals and birds in the park. Many trees are already affected by die back. They are currently being attacked by horses. The park fauna is suffering because trees are dying.

Horse have a place in life but not in our National Park.

SAMPLE 3

Horses shouldn't be allowed in National Parks. Just because some people own horses doesn't mean they can have free rides and food in our park.

Horses spread grasses when they leave their manure. Horses destroy trees. Horses can bite people who go to the park for a picnic. Horses can stand on your foot or kick you and that would be painful. When dogs chase horses there could be a problem because horses bolt. When horses leave their manure, flies breed in it and cause picnic people to spend their time keeping the flies off the food.

SAMPLE 4

Horses are a nuisance.

You have to feed horses all the time and clean their stalls. My mum rides them in the park on Sundays so that's all right by me. I don't have to put up with them at home and there's less cleaning up to do. I wish they could all live in a National Park and then the rangers could look after them and I wouldn't have to. I had a pony once but it died. Horses should be allowed in the park.

The students selected text 2 as the most successful and were able to formulate some rules for writing a persuasive exposition. Language features were also discussed.

The following samples of the discussion demonstrate students' understanding of expository writing:

In number 2 the first sentence introduces the topic clearly and you know what the author's position is straight away.

Every paragraph starts with a topic sentence and then adds evidence to prove it.

The vocabulary sounds like the writer really knows about these things.

The writer doesn't say I at all, just states the supposed facts which is a very clever thing to do because it's as if he/she expects that everyone knows these facts and must agree with his/her case.

Number 1 is just opinions and sounds a bit like slang so people might not take it seriously.

Number 3 is really a list not a logical argument.

Number 4 is a bit of a worry! It's very personal. I think the writer is just bitter about horses because of a nasty experience. I don't think readers would be convinced . They would think it's a bit 'over the top' so if the purpose is to put an argument then it fails.

The teacher listened and wrote comments under two columns, Positive and Negative. Later children devised their rules for writing. As the unit of study progressed they found many authentic situations for writing expository texts and did so with great enthusiasm.

Planning Frameworks

Children work together to discuss the topic and write key words to help them focus on their arguments and evidence in each section (see pages 138–9).

I don't think it's a very good idea to put the hotel there because:

Nature Reserve
The nature reserve could be a tourist attraction, but the roads would get busier and the animals could get run over on the road. Also the animal could get scared of the noise and the people that tour there could try to touch them. The tourists could also try to pick the flowers there too.

Industrial Estate
The industrial estate wouldn't be a very nice site to see, and if you were on the opposite side in the hotel to the beach you would out your window and see the industrial estate. The industrial site causes pollution too, and the air would smell!

Airport
The airport has good and bad points to it. The planes would fly over the hotel and make alot of noise; but the hotel isn't very far from the airport, and it wouldn't be very far to get from it to the hotel

EXPOSITION - TAKING ONE POINT OF VIEW

STATE PROBLEM AND POINT OF VIEW

ASSERTIONS	EVIDENCE/DATA/REFERENCES
1.	
2.	
3.	

CONCLUSION OR SUMMARY

EXPOSITION - PRESENTING BOTH SIDES

State problem

ARGUMENTS FOR	SUPPORTING EVIDENCE
1.	
2.	
3.	

ARGUMENTS AGAINST	SUPPORTING EVIDENCE
1.	
2.	
3.	

CONCLUSION OR SUMMARY

Assessment and Evaluation of Exposition Writing

The continuum of indicators on the following page traces the development of Exposition writing. Teachers may wish to use the indicators to assess children's control of explanation writing and to identify areas that require attention.

Samples of the combined use of the *Writing: Developmental Continuum* and the continuum for Exposition writing are included on pages 142–3 to show how teachers use a combination of both to evaluate children's writing. It is suggested that samples of work be examined and indicators highlighted. The information provided forms a basis for teaching and enables teachers to help children see how their writing can be improved.

A checklist for Expositions is provided on page 144. This is made up of the indicators for the Extending stage of Exposition writing and can be used as a quick way of assessing children's progress in the writing of Expositions.

EXPOSITION INDICATORS

BEGINNING

Purpose:
The writer:
- discusses reasons for writing

Text Organisation and Content
- Shows little evidence of organisation

Thesis
- writes an opening sentence that reveals personal position, e.g. 'I don't think they should chop down trees.'

Argument
- uses little or no justification for viewpoint

Reiteration or Conclusion
- writes a final statement that may not refer to position taken
- offers no conclusion

Language Features
- writes in language close to speech, e.g. 'I reckon it's not fair…'
- writes from first person point of view

DEVELOPING

Purpose:
The writer:
- discusses reasons for writing

Text Organisation and Content
- attempts the use of an exposition framework

Thesis
- writes opening statement that reveals position to be taken in exposition
- expresses thesis subjectively, e.g. *I think…*

Argument
- includes arguments in an arbitrary manner without classifying or organising logically
- provides some supporting evidence

Reiteration or Conclusion
- concludes with a personal statement, e.g. 'Therefore I don't think it is fair because…'

Language Features
- uses imprecise adjectives or adverbs
- writes using personal viewpoint
- uses simple conjunctions, e.g. *and, then, but*
- writes using language close to speech

CONSOLIDATING

Purpose:
The writer:
- sees writing as a means to an end

Text Organisation and Content
- uses the organisational framework of an exposition
- presents information logically

Thesis
- writes an opening paragraph that provides context and uses generalisation to conceal subjective viewpoint
- attempts to provide some context for argument following

Argument
- provides adequate information in some planned or systematic way
- selects details loosely related to the topic
- attempts to generalise
- includes some personal judgements that lack supporting evidence

Reiteration or Conclusion
- attempts to summarise with a paragraph that substantiates the position adopted

Language Features
- uses an impersonal style
- develops coherence by use of additive conjunctions, such as *too, every, also* and adversative conjunctions, such as *however, although, on the other hand*

EXTENDING

Purpose:
The writer:
- uses writing to persuade others

Text Organisation and Content
- effectively organises relevant information using the framework of an exposition
- demonstrates understanding of the function of each stage of an exposition

Thesis
- writes an opening paragraph that consists of a thesis (or position) followed by a brief summary of the arguments to follow

Argument
- locates and uses relevant information
- provides relevant evidence to support assertions
- plans arguments logically
- generalises to authenticate the argument e.g. 'Vehicles pollute the air.'
- presents each paragraph to state a point and then elaborates
- establishes the relationship between part and whole by introducing and concluding each paragraph to lead from one point to the next

Reiteration or Conclusion
- writes a final paragraph that reiterates the main points with an evaluative conclusion

Language Features
- clearly defines words and selects the most effective words for the context
- maintains point of view
- uses complex logical structures to provide authenticity
- expresses actions as things (nominalisation) to make argument seem more objective, e.g. 'Pollution is caused by cars.'
- conceals personal bias through use of objective language, i.e. uses emotive words objectively, e.g. *concern*
- maintains consistency of tense (usually timeless present), e.g. 'Trucks are ruining…'
- uses a variety of verbs, often in passive voice, e.g. *It is believed… roads are ruined…*
- uses adversatives, e.g. *conversely*
- uses controlling words such as *to begin, similarly, finally*
- uses more complex conjunctions, such as *moreover, furthermore, in fact, for example*

Sample of Exposition writing:

31st March
War is very dangerous
for people There are two side
fighting together.

I think war is horrible
because lots of people die.
I would feel sad if
my father towent to war.

Wars are bad because
people's hand get cut off
or an eye or a leg.
I wish the bombs and
the guns and knives and
aeroplanes and the tanks will
be broken into pieces
and there will be peace.

Early Writing Phase Indicators from Writing: Developmental Continuum highlighted:

The writer:

◆ **uses a small range of familiar text forms**
◆ **chooses topics that are personally significant**
● is beginning to use some informational text structures
◆ **uses basic sentence structures and varies sentence beginnings**
● joins simple sentences (often overusing the same connectors, e.g. 'and', 'then')
◆ **can explain in context, some of the purposes of using writing, e.g. shopping list or telephone messages as a memory aid**
◆ **experiments with words drawn from language experience activities, literature, media and oral language of peers and others**
◆ **begins to develop editing skills**
● adds words to clarify meaning
◆ **attempts to use some punctuation**
● sometimes uses full stops
● sometimes uses a capital letter to start a sentence

Exposition Continuum Indicators (Developing) highlighted:

The writer:

● attempts the use of an exposition framework
● writes opening statement that reveals position to be taken in exposition
● includes arguments in an arbitrary manner without classifying or organising logically
● concludes with a personal statement, e.g. 'Therefore I don't think it is fair because…'
● writes using personal viewpoint
● writes using language close to speech

This page provides an example of the combined use of the *Writing: Developmental Continuum* and the continuum for Exposition writing, to evaluate a sample of writing. It confirms placement on the *Writing: Developmental Continuum* and can be used to assess control of Exposition writing.

Sample of Exposition writing:

> ## Should Firework Be Available On C.I?
>
> Fireworks shouldn't be sold in Christmas Island all year because lots of people may get hurt.
>
> Lots of people wake up early in the morning and want a peaceful sleep in the night but the fireworks keep annoying them.
>
> Fireworks burn houses and when they explode, the bits and pieces fall down and litter all around Christmas Island. Adults and children are playing and cleaners are cleaning, so it is not fair to the cleaners which clean the road.
>
> Fireworks are only important to celebrations like Chinese New Year, Hari Raya and Christmas. So, don't play with fireworks too often or you might end up in the Hospital.

Conventional Writing Phase Indicators from Writing: Developmental Continuum highlighted:

The writer:

- **uses text forms to suit purpose and audience**
- considers the needs of audience and includes background information
- **writes a range of texts forms including stories, reports, procedures and expositions**
- demonstrates the ability to develop a topic
- demonstrates knowledge of differences between narrative and informational text when writing
- **uses a variety of simple, compound and extended sentences**
- **groups sentences containing related information into paragraphs**
- uses a variety of linking words such as and, *so, because, if, next, after, before, first*
- **is beginning to select vocabulary according to the demands of audience and purpose, e.g. uses subject-specific vocabulary**
- **uses proof-reading guide or checklist to edit own or peers' writing**
- **punctuates simple sentences correctly**
- uses capital letters for proper nouns
- uses capital letters to start sentences
- uses capital letters for titles
- uses full stops to end sentences
- selects relevant information from a variety of sources before writing
- uses knowledge of other texts as models for writing

Exposition Continuum Indicators (Consolidating) highlighted:

The writer:

- sees writing as a means to an end
- uses the organisational framework of an exposition
- presents information logically
- writes an opening paragraph that provides context and uses generalisation to conceal subjective viewpoint
- attempts to provide some context for argument following
- provides adequate information in some planned or systematic way
- includes some personal judgments that lack supporting evidence
- attempts to summarise with a paragraph that substantiates the position adopted
- uses an impersonal style

This page provides an example of the combined use of the *Writing: Developmental Continuum* and the continuum for Exposition writing, to evaluate a sample of writing. It confirms placement on the *Writing: Developmental Continuum* and can be used to assess control of Exposition writing.

EXPOSITION CHECKLIST	ALWAYS	SOMETIMES	NOT YET
Purpose: The writer: • uses writing to persuade others **Text Organisation and Content** • effectively organises relevant information using the framework of an exposition • demonstrates understanding of the function of each stage of an exposition *Thesis* • writes an opening paragraph that consists of a thesis (or position) followed by a brief summary of the arguments to follow *Argument* • locates and uses relevant information • provides relevant evidence to support assertions • plans arguments logically • generalises to authenticate the argument e.g. 'Vehicles pollute the air.' • presents each paragraph to state a point and then elaborates • establishes the relationship between part and whole by introducing and concluding each paragraph to lead from one point to the next *Reiteration or Conclusion* • writes a final paragraph that reiterates the main points with an evaluative conclusion **Language Features** • clearly defines words and selects the most effective words for the context • maintains point of view • uses complex logical structures to provide authenticity • expresses actions as things (nominalisation) to make argument seem more objective, e.g. 'Pollution is caused by cars.' • conceals personal bias through use of objective language, i.e. uses emotive words objectively, e.g. *concern* • maintains consistency of tense (usually timeless present), e.g. 'Trucks are ruining...' • uses a variety of verbs, often in passive voice, e.g. 'It is believed...' 'roads are ruined...' • uses adversatives, e.g. *conversely* • uses controlling words such as *to begin, similarly, finally* • uses more complex conjunctions such as *moreover, furthermore, in fact, for example*			

Chapter 9:

Teaching Grammar

What is Grammar?

The word Grammar has inherited many meanings. In the field of Linguistics, the term is often used to include everything speakers know about their language: this encompasses phonology (the sound system); semantics (the system of meanings); morphology (the rules of word formation); syntax (the rules of sentence formation); and the lexicon (vocabulary of words).

For various reasons, however, schools have traditionally focused more on the syntactic and morphological aspects of Grammar, preferring to deal with the other aspects under the headings of Spelling, Reading or Word Study.

With this in mind, Grammar is defined in this context as the systematic relationships that exist between the features of the English language. Punctuation is included and is interpreted as the use of standardised marks in writing to clarify meaning.

How Can We Develop Children's Understandings About Grammar?

Learning about grammar and punctuation is a developmental process enhanced by a child's involvement in meaningful language experiences.

Children need to:

- understand that grammar and punctuation conventions are a means to the end of effective writing
- be immersed in an environment rich in language conventions
- be exposed to positive models of use of conventions in both oral and written language
- write for a real purpose and audience
- have the opportunity to test hypotheses and apply appropriate skills in the context of meaningful language on a daily basis
- be able to talk about their language use without being burdened by abstract terminology and complex relationships
- recognise the role of various conventions in relation to particular forms
- have the opportunity to generate rules for the application of conventions
- be aware of a versatile range of editing and proof-reading strategies
- accept responsibility for the editing and proof reading of their work
- monitor their understanding and use of conventions in writing

How Can We Teach Grammar?

The strategies employed in the teaching of grammar and punctuation can be arbitrarily divided into two groups. The first includes strategies that are often integral parts of the writing process. The second involves methods like cloze activities and exercises that are removed from the writing process and are discussed in the section titled Whole-part-whole strategies (page 163) which refers to the process of moving from a piece of writing to focus on a specific convention of interest and then returning to the writing to apply the understandings developed.

Each strategy has advantages and should be chosen according to need. The diagram overleaf on page 148 attempts to give an overview of some strategies, and their relationship to the writing process and other planning elements. The strategies used are neither sequential nor exclusive.

AN EFFECTIVE WAY OF TEACHING GRAMMAR

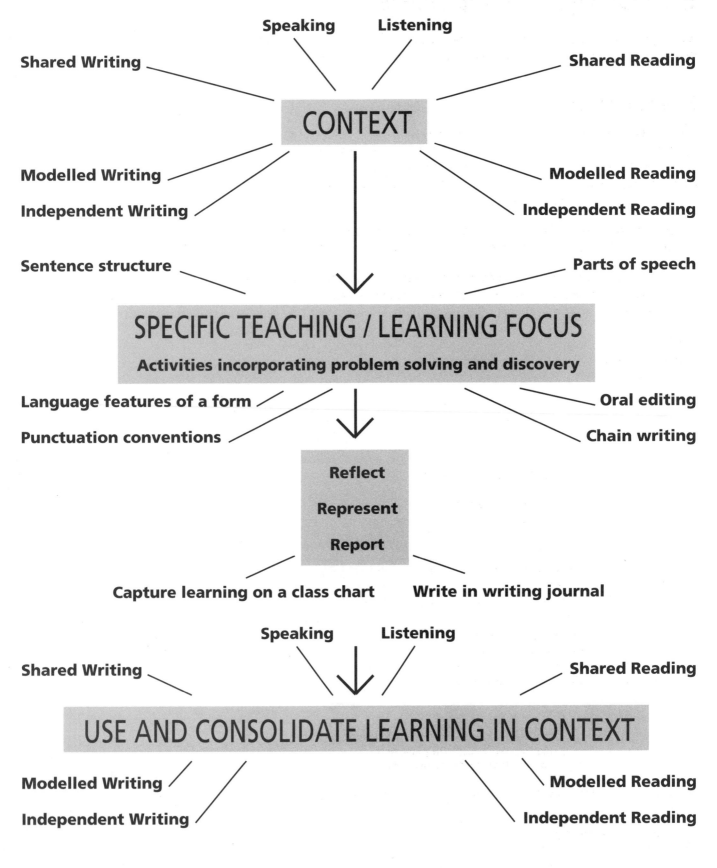

Speaking   Listening

Shared Writing   Shared Reading

CONTEXT

Modelled Writing   Modelled Reading

Independent Writing   Independent Reading

Sentence structure   Parts of speech

SPECIFIC TEACHING / LEARNING FOCUS
Activities incorporating problem solving and discovery

Language features of a form   Oral editing

Punctuation conventions   Chain writing

Reflect
Represent
Report

Capture learning on a class chart   Write in writing journal

Speaking   Listening

Shared Writing   Shared Reading

USE AND CONSOLIDATE LEARNING IN CONTEXT

Modelled Writing   Modelled Reading

Independent Writing   Independent Reading

Teaching Grammar in Context— Exploring the Options

Although most of the strategies explored here are familiar to teachers, their role in the teaching of grammar and punctuation may not be.

Environmental Print

Environmental print is print that is part of everyday life in the form of advertising, signs, street names, maps, calendars, road signs, directions, trademarks, labels, packaging, timetables and so on. This definition extends to include print sources within the classroom, be they planned or incidental, and takes into account a wide range of charts, labels and word banks.

Much of the early literacy learning of young children is fostered as they come to recognise, and in many instances respond to, real language around them.

Advanced writers, too, use environmental print in various ways. For example, many experienced writers, unsure of the punctuation of business letters, check the conventions used in incoming mail.

Teachers can extend the foundation provided by environmental print by:

* Demonstrating the use of environmental print as a resource for learning about conventions. After examining a shared text, children offered the following rules for the use of commas.

Commas are used to:

* **Separate items in a list;**
  eg. Steve walked to the shop to buy meat, salad, bread and soft drink for the barbecue.

* **Separate a word or words used for further explanation;**
  eg. His dog, an excitable bull terrier, decided to wander behind him.

* **Separate the person spoken to from the rest of the sentence;**
  eg. "Steve, I think you have a willing helper," chuckled the store manager.

The chart we developed helps me work out whether I need to use a comma.

* Ensuring that environmental print in the classroom has a meaningful context, e.g. Use labels with a message;

| PLEASE CLOSE THE DOOR | not | DOOR |

- Using environmental print as a stimulus for discussion.

> # burgerboy
> ### The meat to please you.

Most names begin with a capital letter, but in this advertisement a lower case letter is used. Where else does that occur? Why is it written in that way?

- Using the creation of classroom print as a teaching strategy, e.g. *If most of the key words in our Science procedure are verbs, why don't we sort them into alphabetical order and add them to our word bank?*
- Ensuring a wide range of environmental print is available for children to use. By regularly changing the displays in learning centres, shop corners or science tables and taking children on community walks, teachers are able to introduce children to subject-specific vocabulary and a variety of forms and conventions.
- Giving praise to those students who engage with environmental print to solve their own problems in the course of writing.
- Encouraging children to display their favourite sentences from literature they have read.

> "Who's that trip-trapping over my bridge?"

- Using the technique of written replies when responding to the writing of early writers.

> I seen the puppets yesterday.
> I saw the puppets too, Joshua. Did you see anything else?

By replying in this manner the teacher is modelling the correct use of conventions and motivating the student to elaborate on the piece of writing. It is possible for such a strategy to develop into a written conversation which has enormous benefits for the child's understanding of conventions and willingness to write.

Shared Book Experience

The interaction occurring during shared book experience makes it a prime opportunity for the discussion of conventions featured in the text. For younger children this experience provides the stimulus for the use of new and interesting punctuation marks and sentence patterns set in a backdrop of attractive literature. A similar value exists for older children, with the added benefit of providing a forum for the revision of taught concepts and clarification of usage.

Generally, the shared book experience is undertaken in three stages:

1   The book is read purely for enjoyment. Emphasis is given to the characters, the plot, the rhythm or the rhyme. Although the text and pictures are clearly visible to the children, teacher instruction and questioning is kept to a minimum and any discussion is motivated by the interests of the children.

2   If the book is popular, there is little doubt the children will request it again in the days to follow. Within the context of re-reading, the teacher is able to, among many other things, take advantage of curiosity about (for example) the large number of exclamation marks used or the repetition of a particular sentence pattern. An opportunity may arise where a punctuation cloze procedure could be used to stimulate discussion about the function of different forms of punctuation. Similarly, small removable stickers could be used to show how inflectional endings like *ed* and *s* can change the tense and meaning of the story. Vital to the continued success of strategies used in such a golden moment is that they be implemented sparingly and where the need is apparent.

3   The third stage of the shared book experience is optional and flexible. Often children, either alone or in groups, are encouraged to re-read the book in personal reading time.

N.B.   Many publishers include details of the conventions featured in their literature in support material. This allows teachers to co-ordinate a focus for both reading and writing.

> Can you tell me, can you tell me,
> What the builders are doing?
> They are building, they are building,
> So I will build too.

> Can you tell me, can you tell me,
> What the cleaners are doing?
> They are clean …, they are clean …,
> So I will … too.

> Shared book can be used to introduce many concepts and conventions of print, however it should be remembered that the main purpose of sharing literature is enjoyment and the teaching of conventions should not detract from this.

Text Innovations

Many of the conventions exposed and discussed in the Shared Book Experience section have the potential to be direct models for children through Text Innovation. Modelling of rhyme, repetition and a wealth of sentence patterns comes naturally to children as it is the way in which they first learned to talk. Teachers of all year levels can harness the natural willingness to form appealing parts and devices of language. In doing so the teacher is encouraging the child to experiment with theories and apply skills in the context of real language.

Adding to the benefit of the manipulation of an attractive sentence pattern or convention is the fact that the rhyme and repetition involved often begs to be read, chanted or recited aloud. The resulting intonation and expression give yet another dimension to a child's understanding of how grammar and punctuation contribute to a text. Role Play, Experimental and Early Phase writers can gain valuable understandings and task practice of the use of language patterns. Try this:

What Are Little Boys Made Of?
What are little boys made of, made of?
What are little boys made of?
Frogs and snails, and puppy dogs' tails,
That's what little boys are made of.

What Are Mums Made Of?
What are happy Mums made of, made of?
What are happy Mums made of?
Milo and rugs, and warm loving hugs,
That's what Mums are made of.

Conventional and Proficient Phase writers can continue to innovate, only in more sophisticated ways. Innovating on the popular mix and match books allows children to manipulate sentence patterns and become familiar with parts of speech and punctuation marks within the context of an enjoyable activity. The end result is an entertaining, individualised, child-made book boasting thousands of stories made possible by the combination of sentence fragments.

The three sentences below can be accompanied by illustrations that match sentence parts, thereby complementing the written mismatch and enhancing the text. Each line is written on an individual strip, allowing phrases and clauses to mix, e.g.

My energetic teacher
is keen to
climb mountains
in Nepal.

My crazy dog
loves to
chase seagulls
at the beach.

Our class frog
tries to
swallow flies
on the window sill.

My uncle Jim
wants to
lasso buffalo
in the Northern Territory.

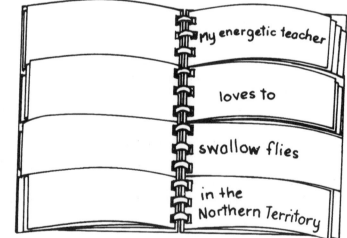

Language Experience

Language experience writing deserves prominence in the teaching of conventions due to the connections it makes between the experience, the oral language and the written product. In the writing and later re-reading of group or class experience work, the young child has the opportunity to develop concepts of print and gradually build an awareness of the functions of words and symbols. The teacher acts as a scribe, producing print from the sentences offered by children to describe the experience. The text must be shaped by the children and in their ownership they help make decisions about the use of conventions.

Important features of language experience include:

- planning language events that will interest children
- seizing the opportunity when a spontaneous event—like major earthworks nearby interrupting your maths test—allows you to capitalise on the natural, enthusiastic oral and written language of the children
- allowing the children to control the extent of revising and editing
- publishing the finished product attractively to encourage personal re-readings
- making the published copy available for other language activities

Modelled Writing

Modelled writing is a simple but effective strategy for teaching the use of language conventions. When the teacher takes on the role of author and demonstrates the many aspects of the writing process, the child is able to see how each challenge is confronted and met. For example, the thinking aloud that goes into deciding whether to use a question mark or an exclamation mark reveals to the child a generalisation that may be used to solve a similar problem in the child's future writing.

Modelled writing sessions allow the teacher to emphasise those conventions required by the children at that particular time. Most importantly, modelled writing shows children the direct relationship between thorough revision and editing, and effective writing.

Daily Writing

Daily writing is defined here as the discrete 15–20 minute session of uninterrupted writing teachers often employ as distinct from the lengthier process of moving a piece of writing from draft to publication. It is sometimes titled *Uninterrupted Sustained Silent Writing*.

Daily writing provides excellent opportunities to:

- allow children to get the regular practice they need in applying conventions
- generate drafts for writing
- encourage children to test theories about writing in a safe situation

Sentence Manipulation

Research has indicated that sentence manipulation plays a large part in the development of writers. Many children battle first with the concept of a sentence and then with the control of its obvious flexibility. Time spent on sentence manipulation activities, all of which are easily linked to a writing focus, is invaluable to the developing writer. Shared literature, individual writing excerpts and text from newstelling provide an authentic context for these activities. The following can be used with whole class, small group or individual children.

Sentence Makers

Whether commercial or self-made, sentence makers have the infinite potential of the sentence itself. A simple holding strip and a handful of cards bearing words can lead to a range of activities that can be conducted on a class, group or individual basis.

For example:

- Basic sentence making.
  Allow the children to construct sentences at will, using news sessions and exciting events, favourite books and word banks to stimulate their choice of words.

- Sentence expansion.
  Use the sentence maker to extend existing sentences by inserting additional adjectives, adverbs, phrases and clauses.

- Sentence reduction.
  Use the sentence maker to reduce a long sentence to its simplest form by removing one word at a time. This activity is much more difficult than the preceding one as the sentence must be re-read each time to see if it still makes sense. It is important to recognise that beginning writers usually need to add relevant information while more advanced authors benefit from the reduction or tightening of sentences.

- Sentence transformation.
  Use the sentence maker to transform a sentence by taking turns to change one word at a time. A noun must be changed for a noun, a verb for a verb and so on. Decide whether nonsense will be allowed. For instance:

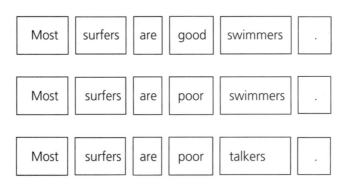

- Matching sentence parts.
  Copy a series of sentences from a popular story or book onto card strips. Cut the strips into individual word cards and mix them up. Have the children match them up to make sense or nonsense.

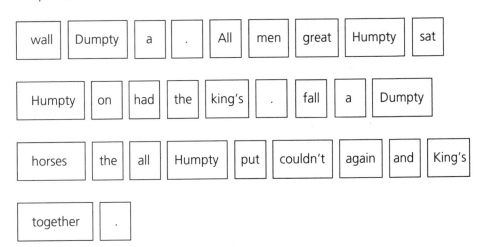

| wall | Dumpty | a | . | All | men | great | Humpty | sat |

| Humpty | on | had | the | king's | . | fall | a | Dumpty |

| horses | the | all | Humpty | put | couldn't | again | and | King's |

| together | . |

- Sentence completion.
  Make a series of sentence beginnings or sentence endings and let the children invent the missing part. This activity takes on extra importance when conjunctions are used.

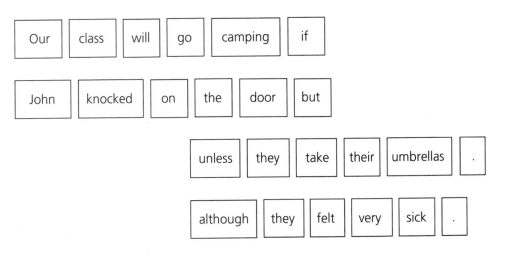

| Our | class | will | go | camping | if |

| John | knocked | on | the | door | but |

| unless | they | take | their | umbrellas | . |

| although | they | felt | very | sick | . |

- Sentence modelling.
  Use a familiar sentence pattern from a shared text as the basis for the construction of more sentences.

- Sentence comparison.
  By rewriting the text using the children's own language and discussing the two (or more) different forms, the teacher provides a focus point for a discussion of how word order affects meaning and how sentences may be re-arranged to become more appealing.

| ' | No | , | no | , | no | , | ' | said | the | village |

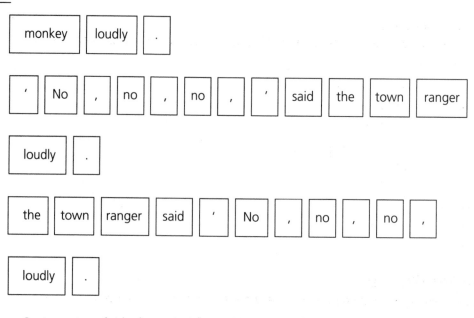

| monkey | loudly | . |

| ' | No | , | no | , | no | , | ' | said | the | town | ranger |

| loudly | . |

| the | town | ranger | said | ' | No | , | no | , | no | , |

| loudly | . |

- Sentence transformation : singular to plural (or vice versa).
  Discuss the changes necessary when the subject of the sentence becomes plural.

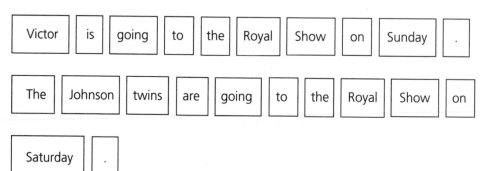

| Victor | is | going | to | the | Royal | Show | on | Sunday | . |

| The | Johnson | twins | are | going | to | the | Royal | Show | on |

| Saturday | . |

- Sentence transformation: tenses.
  Compare the construction of the sentence in the three main tenses.

Present

| I | am | catching | tadpoles | . |

Past

| I | caught | tadpoles | . |

Future

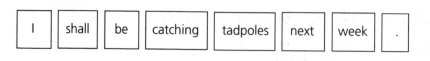

| I | shall | be | catching | tadpoles | next | week | . |

156

- Sentence stems.
  Manipulate sentence structure to enhance the meaning of the sentence stem provided.

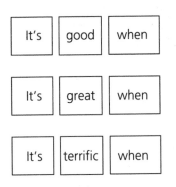

It's	good	when
It's	great	when
It's	terrific	when

Chain Writing

Chain writing is the name given to the gradual expansion of a sentence.

1 Select a word related to the theme you are developing, e.g. spiders.

2 Ask the children to suggest words which describe spiders, e.g.

hairy
scary
black
sneaky   *spiders*
horrible
long-legged

3 Then ask what spiders do and add the words to the list, e.g.

hairy   *climb*
scary   *hide*
black   *lurk*
sneaky   *spiders*   *creep*
horrible   *bite*
long-legged   *sleep*

4 Now combine the words to make sentences such as

Hairy spiders creep.
Black spiders hide.
Horrible spiders bite.

5 Next list where spiders do things and add these to the list:

hairy   *climb*   *in the garden*
scary   *hide*   *in the bathroom*
black   *lurk*   *under the wood pile*
sneaky   *spiders*   *creep*   *inside the light shade*
horrible   *bite*   *in their webs*
long-legged   *sleep*   *on the pergola*

and combine as before to make different sentences, e.g.

Long-legged spiders sleep in the bathroom.
Scary spiders lurk inside the light shade.

6 Other questions can be asked to elicit additional responses, e.g. when?

at night
during the day
just before dawn
every day
once a week

why?

to find food
just for fun
to find a friend
to stay warm
because it's a habit

7 Sentences can be written on coloured cards and made into spiral books for reading.

8 Children can be asked to write their own stories about spiders now that they have a wide range of ideas and words to stimulate their imaginations. You may like to look for or create poetry within the sentences.

Physical Sentence Reconstruction

The obvious extension of chain writing and sentence making is to list words and phrases on individual cards and use them for sentence creation and reconstruction. This is best achieved by asking individual children to be responsible for one card each. As a group, the children involved must arrange themselves in an order that makes sense.

The advantages of such an exercise are:

- A large number of children become involved.
- Weaker children find assistance in the guidance of their classmates.
- Children start to realise the relationships between words, e.g. In every sentence we make, Martin, who has the word hairy, stands on the left hand side of Ricky, who has the word spider.

- Judgements can be made about the most appropriate sentence for the context, e.g. *Which sentence fits best?*
Hairy spiders creep in the garden every day.
or
Every day hairy spiders creep in the garden.
or
In the garden hairy spiders creep every day.
or
In the garden every day hairy spiders creep.

Sentence Diagrams

Sentence manipulation need not always be a formal activity. The conversation below could be part of a one-to-one conference, a group conference or a class focus on sentence expansion.

Bruce's text: We went to the pool.

Teacher:	*Who went to the pool, Bruce?*
Bruce:	*Shelley and I.*
Teacher:	*How could you add that to your Recount?*
Bruce:	*Shelley and I went to the pool.*
Teacher:	*Well done, Bruce! How did you get to the pool?*
Bruce:	*We walked.*
Teacher:	*How could we include that part in your sentence?*
Bruce:	*Shelley and I walked to the pool.*
Teacher:	*Why did you go to the pool, Bruce?*
Bruce:	*Because it was hot at home.*
Teacher:	*Could that be added to your sentence?*
Bruce:	*Shelley and I walked to the pool because it was hot at home.*

We can show these changes, including transformations, reductions, expansions and rearrangements, in a diagram on the blackboard, e.g.

Editing and Proof Reading

Revising, editing and proof reading are three vital, overlapping skills which take a piece of writing from a crude train of thought scribbled down on paper to a tight, clear manuscript ready for publication.

Revising generally refers to changes made to ideas at the paragraph level, editing involves clarifying meaning at the sentence level and proof reading is a final check of punctuation and spelling. Children usually understand proof reading, as it involves tangible elements like capital letters, commas and full stops.

Establishing a respect for the value of editing is somewhat harder and may involve regular sentence manipulation for the result to be appreciated as an improvement of the work. While early writers justifiably can't be expected to show a great deal of interest in the revision of a piece of writing, the teaching of all three skills is paramount to the child's ability to manipulate punctuation and grammar for useful means.

Ways to encourage editing and proof reading include:

- demonstrating techniques in regular modelled writing sessions
- using conferences to impart skills
- modelling positive questioning methods for group or peer conferences
- recommending that children read their work aloud to hear mistakes
- modelling the acceptance of adding, deleting and altering as a messy, but necessary part of revision
- recognising that many readers need to leave a draft for some time to be able to look at it from a new perspective
- limiting early revision experiences to short, easy pieces of writing
- concentrating on only one or two skills at a time
- being aware that most young children learn to revise in the sequence: add, cut and re-order
- supplying helpful editors' checklists
- encouraging the use of computer word processing packages and concept keyboard overlays where they encourage good habits

Passages for Editing and Proof Reading

When considering texts to be used for demonstrating editing and proof reading, the following factors should be kept in mind:

- any child's work should only be used with the child's permission; nevertheless, commentary about the work should focus on the positive aspects first and assume the tone of a constructive peer conference, relying primarily on guiding questions and respecting the author's ownership
- passages produced by the teacher to highlight a teaching point should be economical in terms of clarifying a focus, but should have a connection to an authentic language context
- children relate well to a piece of writing written by an author of similar development because they can relate to the struggles and similarities of the writing process
- literature excerpts should be used sparingly and the literary value of the piece preserved

Oral Editing

Oral editing has merit at all developmental levels. Many children can hear pauses in their own reading as indicators of full stops and soon become aware of how their intonation might signal an exclamation mark or comma. One procedure for oral editing is given below:

1 Choose a child, e.g. Christine, an Early Phase writer who is reading and writing with confidence but does not know how to punctuate her stories correctly.
2 Ask Christine if she would like the class to help her to put the capitals and full stops in the right places.
3 Copy Christine's story onto a large piece of paper (or overhead transparency) and display it so that the whole class can see.
4 Use this enlarged copy during sharing time to model the proof reading strategy you want the children to eventually use by themselves.

- Teacher (or child and teacher) reads the story, stopping at the end of each sentence.
- Class claps when the teacher's voice stops.
- Christine puts in the full stop while the class observes.

- Teacher points out that the next word after the full stop is a new sentence and therefore must begin with a capital.
- Christine changes that letter to a capital while everyone watches.
- Continue along these lines until the whole story has been read.
- Leave this enlarged story pinned up so that children can refer to it and even practise the strategy with a partner.

This method of editing evolves into a child-owned technique and becomes more powerful as this occurs.

> If a child has no interest in the purpose, form or audience of a piece of writing, no amount of revising, editing or proof reading on the part of the author will improve it.

Problem-solving Approach to Teaching Conventions

In using the problem-solving approach to teaching conventions, children are shown models of writing forms. By analysing these models children are able to identify the prominent conventions and generate rules for their application.

For example, year six students might read three business letters that have been sent to their class in response to requests for sponsorship for an annual camp. Apart from many other conventions, the large number of capitals employed in this form would allow the students to categorise the capital letters according to how they are used. A typical discussion might follow the lines of:

T: How many capitals are there in this business letter?
C: Nineteen.
T: Are they all used for the same reason?
C: Most of them are for names of streets and places.
C: Some are for the names of people.
T: Are there any others?
C: Lots of the capitals are used to start a sentence.
C: And for things like 'Dear' and 'Yours sincerely'.
T: Let's make a chart of different purposes for capital letters.

Chart can be displayed for future reference.

At least four logical sequels to this lesson could build on the understanding of how and when capital letters are employed:

- Future forms of text encountered in any subject could be examined on an informal basis to see whether any new categories can be added to the chart, e.g. 'Why does this book use capitals for God and Him and He?'
- Students could examine a similar form altered by the teacher—in this instance a business letter—and try to identify where capitals need to be added and for what reason. Editing decisions could be discussed in groups and consensus reached.
- Students could write in the form displayed, employing the awareness they have recently gained. Writing more requests or replies in reference to the annual camp would provide an ideal context for a true test of their skills.
- Use the chart as a ready reference, and if necessary, update or modify.

The strength of the Problem-Solving Approach rests in the critical analysis of how conventions are used and the application of child-made theories of language.

Linking Forms and Conventions

Where possible the writing of a form of text should be linked to the teaching of a convention. Not only is the integrity of the language encounter maintained or even enhanced, but some children are also able to recall the syntactic features of a form when it is necessary to use that form again. Similarly many conventions adopt different roles, depending on the form in which they are employed, e.g.

List adjectives to describe spiders.

> horrible
> gruesome
> ugly

(These adjectives would be inappropriate in an informational text.)

If children are to examine the emphasis of a syntactic convention in a form, it is best that they have an understanding of the form first. Where unfamiliar forms are employed the whole text conventions should be taught and understood first.

An awareness of the conventions prominent in a wide range of text forms adds versatility to the language programme. Consider the grammatical features that may be taught from the following forms:

Births

MOUSE (nee Skirt):

Micky and Minnie are proud to announce the arrival of a cute daughter, Murgatroyd, on 17.5.91. Thanks to Dr Skill and staff at M.F.I.H.

Road Worker

Husky hands,
Black boots,
Pneumatic drill,
Grey concrete,
No power.

Flood

'*Flood, flood!*' shouts Mr Mud.

'*Where, where?*' cries Mrs Care.

'*In the street,*' says Mr Feet.

'*Save my house!*' pleads Ms Grouse.

'*No time,*' weeps Mrs Grime.

'*What'll we do?*' screams Mr Magoo.

'*Climb a tree,*' yells Dr Fee.

'*I hate heights!*' squeals Mr Knights.

'*Where's the boat,*' screams Mr Grote.

Whole-part-whole Strategies

Whole-part-whole strategies rely on explicit links with the text in progress. For this reason the links should be obvious in terms of time and content. Children should be aware of the rationale of each activity and how it should help their writing.

Cloze

Widespread use of the cloze procedure as a reading strategy is an indication of the technique's simplicity and value. That worth is duplicated when cloze is considered as a tool for teaching grammar and punctuation and multiplied when children are allowed to discuss their answers with their peers. Some of the possibilities are listed below:

Controlled Cloze

Cloze used as a teaching strategy for reading inevitably aids the understanding of grammar as children come to understand that certain words are acceptable within the structure of the sentence while others may sound and look awkward, e.g.

The strawberries **is** ripe when they turn a bright red colour.

Where necessary cloze exercises taken from an interesting piece of text can be constructed to focus on a specific syntactic form e.g. to encourage children to maintain point of view and tense when speaking and writing:

Carol (run, running, ran) to the jetty.

Crazy Cloze

By deleting all of one particular part of speech in a piece of text and asking the children to replace the words without seeing the text, a humorous, if nonsensical, text will result.

Ask the children to list ten adjectives of any sort on a piece of paper, e.g. juicy, plastic, circular, delicious, well-mannered, ugly, floral, cold, sad, disgusting.

Once this has been done, give them a passage that has ten adjectives deleted:

The South Coast Vultures were nothing short of _____ as they steamrolled a _____ Footsplay side at the B.A.C.A. Ground last night. Starting the match without their _____ ruckman, Bruce Kneebone, the Vultures took some time to become accustomed to the _____ conditions before _____ full-forward Keith Moonbeam took a _____ mark in the square and kicked a _____ goal . Later in this _____ game, the ball became _____ and by quarter time the crowd was _____.

Insert the invented adjectives and read aloud. Although the results are predictably hilarious, children are quick to sense any mismatch in the sentence structure. Some children will find their text loses its appeal because some of their words just don't fit. This is an opportune time to redefine the term 'adjective' and clarify any misunderstandings. Others will point out that the passage above includes 'took a ugly mark' and needs to be corrected.

The obvious extension for this type of cloze is to allow the children to develop sensible alternatives to the chosen adjectives. However, having the children construct their own cloze passages is another option.

Punctuation Cloze

Proof reading activities which require children to supply all the necessary punctuation are a difficult proposition for developing writers. Just as readers require a certain number of clues to decipher the general meaning of a cloze passage, writers need clues about the organisation of sentences and punctuation. One way of doing this is to provide dashes or boxes to indicate where punctuation should be. For example

> Why are we moving house_ Gerry asked his mother _ The expression on her face was answer enough_ He placed his new computer game_ baseball glove and chess set carefully into the packing box and walked outside_

Punctuation cloze is best completed first by individuals and later justified in groups. Interaction of this sort is essential to allow children to model from the strategies of the more able students, and to develop an awareness of the alternative answers possible for some of the blanks. This strategy can be adapted by using removable stickers to cover key pieces of punctuation in a shared book session.

Oral Cloze

Yet another adaptation of this strategy is to produce certain sounds to represent specific punctuation symbols, e.g. full stop … snap fingers; question mark … whistle. Groups could be asked to punctuate a volunteer's writing with their chosen sounds, while the task of the audience is to guess which sounds are representing which punctuation symbols.

Games

Although the role of games in teaching grammar and punctuation is normally one of revision or consolidation, many opportunities arise for their use in the initial teaching of concepts.

For example, in teaching children that there are degrees of adjectives (positive, comparative and superlative), rather than providing the children with a stencil which requires completion of relevant exercises, the teacher could play a modified game of I Spy, e.g. 'I spy with my little eye something that is *smaller* than a desk, but *larger* than a ruler.' A written riddle incorporating the same concept would be an ideal extension of this game.

Similarly, games in other subjects offer many possibilities. The same concept of degrees of adjectives could be developed within a mathematics lesson where children arrange objects from the largest to the smallest.

Coffee Pot

This simple game involves one member of the class or of each group being sent outside while a verb is chosen. For example, the nominated word could be *laugh*. When the isolated member of the class or group returns to the class, he/she must ask questions to identify the verb; they do this by substituting *coffee pot* (or some other meaningless noun) for the unknown verb, e.g. 'Do dogs *coffee pot*? Replies are limited to *yes* or *no*.

Name Game

After introducing the class to the simple sentence pattern *proper noun-verb-adverb* (Carol creeps carefully) it is possible to consolidate the parts of speech and the relationship between each by playing the Name Game. Following a sequence, students must provide a word that follows the pattern set for the sentence. For example, player one says *Daniel*, player two says *drives* and player three says *dangerously*; the pattern then begins again. If a player is unable to call out a word that fits the sentence, they sit down and so the process of elimination continues. This game is not easy, but would become more involved with practice. Numerous variables exist which can be controlled or adapted to suit the purpose of the game. Will the class accept *Frank photographs furiously*? Does the sentence have to make sense? Is it possible to have a verb that can't be followed by an adverb? The game could be made more complex by adding a noun element and might benefit from the best sentences being written down for display, e.g. *Frank photographs fish furiously*.

Alphabet Loop

An adaptation of the Name Game is to allow any sentence structure as long as the words of the sentence follow each letter of the alphabet, e.g. **A**ll **b**lack **c**ats **d**rink **e**gg **f**lips. The benefits of this game would include the consideration of alternatives for sentence beginnings and the discussion that would develop in deciding what constitutes a sentence.

Wordback Spied Her

In this physical word sort, students have words pegged to their backs. Individuals move around the room with a given list (spelling list, vocabulary list, etc.) from which their word comes and ask questions like, *Is it a noun?* or *Does it have a suffix?* Questions may only be answered *yes* or *no*. Problem-solving skills are developed and understanding of parts of speech is reinforced.

Semantic Grid

The semantic grid is a versatile and popular reading comprehension strategy with potential for revision of parts of speech. For example, having read an expository text dealing with health, the children could be asked to draw on their own knowledge and the information provided by the text to complete the grid below. First correct entry wins!

	H	E	A	L	T	H
Noun	*heart*			*lungs*		
Verb		*eat*			*train*	
Adjective			*active*			*healthy*

Be sure to discuss the fact that one word may fall into more than one category, depending on the context in which it is used, e.g. no *added* sugar (adjective), he *added* sugar (verb).

Computer Programs

Versatile computer software incorporating grammar and punctuation concepts are a bonus to the busy teacher. Faced with the task of meeting the needs of a wide range of students, the teacher may be able to direct individuals, pairs or carefully managed small groups to an attractive program that suits their needs. The advantages of such a strategy include:

- the motivation of working with a computer
- the independence of the workers
- the flexibility inherent in many computer programs

To gain maximum benefit from computer programs, the area of focus should be firmly embedded in a purposeful language context and the limits of the program acknowledged. A package intended for testing or revision of conventions will not serve a teaching purpose.

Exercises

Despite having accrued a poor reputation as the sole avenue for teaching grammar and punctuation in purposeful classrooms, textbook exercises may still have a role to play in the present teaching of conventions. As long as the connection between the language context and the exercise is clearly a purposeful one, there is no reason to disregard commercial texts or teacher-made exercises.

Exercises need to be:

- used sparingly
- carefully assessed to ascertain their value to the language task
- imitations of tasks real writers undertake

What Needs to be Taught?

In deciding what and when to teach, teachers should be guided by both the individual needs of the children and the skills that foster an improvement in the children's language.

The individual needs of a student can be assessed in the short term by regular conferences and in the long term by use of the *Writing Developmental Continuum*. Both will indicate when a child is mature enough to recognise and understand the contribution of the skill(s) in their writing.

Where a large group or class can benefit from the introduction of a new convention, the scope and sequence chart beginning on page 167 is offered as a guide.

Key: E - Exposure, T -Teaching, M - Maintenance

Punctuation

	K-1	2-3	4-5	6-7
Full stops				
use of full stops to end statements, e.g. Writing is fun.	E/T	T	M	M
use of full stops in initials, e.g. W.D. Murphy, W.A.	E	E	T	M
use of full stops in abbreviations (those that do not end in the final letter of the word), e.g. Mon., Dec., Sec.	E	E	T	M
N.B. Full stops are not required after titles, dates (unless at the end of a sentence), measurement symbols and abbreviations that end with the final letter of the word.				
Capital letters				
use of capital letters to begin sentences, e.g. Writing takes time.	E/T	T	M	M
use of capital letters for proper nouns (names, days, months, places, titles, streets), e.g. Susan, Tuesday, February, Indonesia, Captain Cook, Victoria Street.	E/T	E	T	M
use of capital letters for adjectives derived from proper nouns, e.g. Indonesian.	E/T	E	M	M
use of capital letters for the pronoun I.	E	T	M	M
use of capital letters for book titles, first word in a line of poetry, e.g. Gulliver's Travels, Slowly the river rises	E/T	E	T	M
use of capital letters for emphasis, e.g. HAPPY BIRTHDAY!	E	T	M	M
use of capital letters for names of deity, special days, names of institutions, e.g. *God, Boxing Day, Brunswick Primary School.*	E	T	M	M
N.B. Capital letters are not necessary for points of the compass (unless forming part of a title) and seasons of the year.				
Question marks				
use of question marks at the end of sentences that ask for information, e.g. Why are we doing this?	E/T	T	M	M
N.B. Question marks are not needed: (i) when using indirect speech, e.g. The captain was asked if he was fit to play. (ii) when a sentence is a request, e.g. Can you hurry up.				
Exclamation marks				
use of exclamation marks to show strong feeling, e.g. What a mess!	E/T	T	T	M

	K-1	2-3	4-5	6-7
Commas				
use of commas:				
to separate items in a series, e.g. They collected shells, driftwood, coral and cuttlefish. N.B. The items may be nouns, verbs, adjectives or groups of words.	E	ET	M	M
to separate a word/words used in a sentence for further explanation, e.g. Mary, the golden haired girl, won the medal.		E	T	T
before joining words when they join two main clauses, e.g. He wanted to travel to China, but he wanted to learn the language first.			E	T
to separate main and subordinate clauses, e.g. When they heard the final siren, the players leapt into the air.		E	T	M
to separate the person spoken to from the rest of the sentence, e.g. Richard, mind the wet paint.		E	T	M
after words like *yes* and *no*, e.g. No, you can't come in here.		E	T	M
to separate month and year in date, e.g. Thursday, June 27, 1991.		E	T	M
to follow signal words at the beginning of sentences, e.g. However, I believe…			E	T
Apostrophes				
use of apostrophes for contractions, e.g. can't, won't, doesn't	E	T	M	M
use of apostrophes to show ownership, e.g. Barry's holiday, elephants' enclosure.		E	T	M
use of apostrophes to indicate letters or numbers omitted, e.g. 'phone, o'clock, '91. N.B. Apostrophes are not necessary when the noun is descriptive rather than possessive, e.g. mens toilet, teachers notes.		E	T	M
Quotation marks				
use of quotation marks when using direct speech, e.g. *"That will do!"* she shouted. N.B. Quotation marks are not used for indirect speech, e.g. Brewhouse told his players to run harder and share the ball.	E	T	T	M
use of quotation marks to show quotations within quotations, e.g. *"My father always* said 'look on the bright side' and I suppose *I do,"* explained Dennis.				E
use of quotation marks before and after titles or words used in an unorthodox manner, e.g. Some viewers actually consider "The Video Show" a form of "entertainment".			E	T

	K-1	2-3	4-5	6-7

Colon

use of colons to:

introduce a list, e.g. Greg packed his drawing gear: pencils, paints, crayons, paper and easel.				E/T
introduce a quotation, e.g. The boss said: "I have some good news for you."				E/T
introduce an explanation, summary or elaboration of the first half of a sentence, e.g. I'm not much of a runner: I tend to cross the pain barrier just getting out of bed.				E/T

Semi-colon

use of semi-colons to:

join sentences with two or more main clauses, e.g. A face appeared at the window; he was one determined animal.			E	E
separate clauses containing commas, e.g. At that point our captain, who had previously remained calm, lost control and stormed off; the game had to be abandoned.			E	E

Hyphen

use of hyphens to:

join some parts of compound words, e.g. father-in-law, heavy-handed.			E	T
join a group of words to form an expression, e.g. good-for-nothing.			E	T
write numbers and fractions that consist of more than one word, e.g. five-sixths, forty-nine.			E	T

Dash

use of a dash to:

introduce a list, e.g. The burglar collected his tools—torch, screwdriver, saw and tyre lever.			E	T
create surprise, e.g. She pulled herself to her feet—still prepared to fight.			E	T

Use of Sentences

Write sentences

write sentences containing a main verb, e.g. The child *hit* the ball.	E/T	M	M	M

N.B. Verbs are often called 'doing words' because they describe an action. To make sense a sentence must have a verb.

Join sentences

join sentences using conjunctions, e.g. *and, then, but, because, so, yet, or.*	E	T	M	M

169

Modification of sentences

	K-1	2-3	4-5	6-7
use of adjectives to enhance the meaning of sentences, e.g. The *little* girl hit the *white* ball.	E	T	M	M

N.B. An adjective tells you more about a noun or pronoun. Adjectives are frequently referred to as "describing words".

	K-1	2-3	4-5	6-7
use of adverbs to enhance the meaning of sentences, e.g. The child hit the ball		E	T	M

powerfully.

N.B. An adverb provides more information about a verb, and sometimes adjectives and other adverbs. An adverb often answers the questions: How? When? Where? or Why?

	K-1	2-3	4-5	6-7
demonstrate understanding of function of adjectives		E	T	M
define the term adjective.		E	T	M
demonstrate understanding of function of adverbs		E	T	M
define the term adverb.		E	T	M
identify and use adjectival phrases, e.g. The child *with the strong muscles* hit the ball.			E	T

N.B. A phrase is a group of words which is unable to make sense on its own because it does not contain a verb. Adjectival phrases takes the place of adjectives.

	K-1	2-3	4-5	6-7
identify and use adverbial phrases, e.g. The child hit the ball *to first base*. Adverbial phrases act as adverbs.			E	T
identify and use adjectival clauses, e.g. The child hit the ball *which was thrown by the pitcher*.			E	E/T

N.B. A clause is a group of words which includes a verb. A main clause can stand independently as a sentence, however a subordinate clause (shown above) relies on a main clause for its meaning. An adjectival clause serves as an adjective in a sentence.

	K-1	2-3	4-5	6-7
identify and use adverbial clauses, e.g. The child hit the ball *because he was angry*. An adverbial clause acts as an adverb.				E/T

Isolate subject and predicate

	K-1	2-3	4-5	6-7
isolate subject and predicate in a sentence, e.g. *The huge bird* flew over the fence.			E	T

N.B. The subject is the thing or person featured in the sentence, while the predicate is what is said about the subject.

	K-1	2-3	4-5	6-7
write sentences in which the subject and verb agree in number, e.g. A *packet* of lollies *was* on the table. A *box* of matches *is* small. *The children were* visiting the zoo.				E/T

Parts of Speech

	K-1	2-3	4-5	6-7
Use of pronouns				
write pronouns which are consistent with the number and case of the subject or object to which these pronouns refer, i.e. subject-pronoun agreement, e.g. *The children* watched the game., *They* enjoyed it.		E	T	M

N.B. Pronouns are words referring to a person or thing, e.g. *them, him*

	K-1	2-3	4-5	6-7
write an appropriate pronoun for a previously stated subject or object in order to avoid repetition, e.g. *My Dad* walked into the shop. *He* bought a packet of lollies. The car ran into *the people*. An ambulance took *them* to hospital.	E	T	M	M

Isolate nouns, verbs, adjectives and

adverbs in sentences

	K-1	2-3	4-5	6-7
explain functions of adjectives, nouns, verbs and adverbs in sentences, e.g. The large bird flew gracefully.	E	T	M	M

Avoid repetition

	K-1	2-3	4-5	6-7
write vivid adjectives and explicit nouns to avoid unnecessary repetition of pronouns, e.g. *The lion sprang at the hunter. The angry beast growled horribly. It clawed the man viciously.*	E	T	M	M

not

The lion sprang at the hunter. It growled

It clawed…

Avoid redundancies

	K-1	2-3	4-5	6-7
e.g. My dad *he*…, The train was *more* bigger…	E	T	M	M

Structure of Text

Make alterations:

	K-1	2-3	4-5	6-7
add words to enhance meaning	T	M	M	M
change words to achieve exact description.	E	T	M	M
delete words to tighten sentences.	E	T	M	M
re-arrange words to produce a more convincing order.		E	T	M
add phrases to enhance meaning of sentences.	E	T	M	M
re-arrange sentences to produce a more convincing sequence.		E	T	M
write paragraphs appropriate to the structure of the form.		E	T	M
re-arrange paragraphs to produce a more convincing order.				E

Adapted from: *Programming Ideas K-7*, Volume 5 (1985) Ministry of Education, Western Australia.

Chapter 10

Helping Children Who Have Writing Difficulties

Introduction

Probably everyone at some time or other has difficulty with writing. However, children who are learning to write have to overcome the difficulties of holding the pen, recognising and forming letters and words, spelling, sentence construction, punctuation and whole text structure while still concentrating on translating thoughts into writing to suit the purpose and intended audience. When these complexities are added to some school situations—where writing is often done in a limited time, because it's timetabled, about a topic which is of little interest to the writer, to be read by someone who is likely to be more interested in how the writing is constructed than what is written—then it is easy to understand why some children find writing an onerous task. This chapter outlines some suggestions for helping children who have difficulties with writing. The suggestions reflect an approach which involves the child, teacher, school and parents in helping to provide a suitable instructional program.

The development of the skill of handwriting is not specifically addressed in this chapter. Whilst appreciating that the knowledge of letter shapes, spacing and directionality are important aspects of writing, teachers will understand that the most important aim of writing is to develop, in children, an interest in writing and to help them understand the purposes for which it is used. Aspects of handwriting such as pencil hold, posture, letter formation and so on, should be developed within the context of writing. Special attention may be paid to individual children, small instructional groups or whole class focuses to improve the hand–eye coordination, use of spacing, directionality, pencil skills or visual memory of letter shapes in order to the improve legibility of children's written language The use of computers or typewriters is another option to consider.

There are many possible causes of children's writing problems. Children may have started in an environment that was uncaring or ignorant of their needs or have had one or more bad experiences with writing. These children are not 'poor writers' but somewhere on the *Writing: Developmental Continuum*. This chapter focuses on the gathering of data to accurately diagnose the nature of children's difficulties and promotes the belief that the instructional program must focus on developing the skills, strategies and attitudes that are essential for a child's writing development.

A Whole School Approach

Children who are experiencing writing difficulties need to:

- have the opportunity to learn to write by writing
- have the opportunity to talk about their writing experiences
- experience success and develop confidence in themselves as writers
- have more time to develop
- see writing as enjoyable and worthwhile
- be aware of their own strategies
- be aware of others' strategies
- be encouraged to take control of their own learning

Teachers helping children who have writing difficulties need to:

- gather information about children's writing development across a range of writing activities where children are working in different contexts
- use a diagnostic approach to identify the child's developing knowledge, understandings, skills and strategies
- use diagnostic information to identify appropriate teaching strategies
- keep natural language teaching principles in mind when planning, e.g. writing and reading are interrelated
- plan an instructional program that builds on the child's strengths and ensures success
- use a variety of approaches
- ensure that there is a balance between explicit and general instruction
- provide many opportunities for children to practise and apply their skills and strategies
- model all skills and strategies involved in writing
- provide support in the context of the regular classroom (plan for whole class, small group and individual activities)
- provide ready access to support materials such as reference charts made with children, word banks, dictionaries, books, children's writing

Schools need to:

- develop a policy that outlines beliefs in relation to supporting children who have writing difficulties
- identify children at risk and monitor their development as they progress through the school
- ensure school timetables allow large blocks of time to enable class teachers to implement a language program to meet the need of all children in the class
- ensure that there is some continuity in the approach used to support children who have writing difficulties
- select resources that will support children who are having writing difficulties
- provide professional development opportunities for teachers

Parents helping children with writing difficulties need:

- to have a clear understanding of the school's beliefs in relation to supporting children who have writing difficulties
- to know how they can support their child's writing development at home
- to attend parent–teacher interviews where the developmental continuum can be used to focus on their child's strengths, developing knowledge, understandings skills and strategies
- to have access to parent information sessions

Suggested Pathway for Intervention

Step 1
Gather Data

Information should be gathered across a range of writing activities.

Assessment activities may include the following:

- Talking to the child about writing and showing a positive interest in the child's efforts
- Observation and analysis of children's writing behaviours before, during and after writing during regular classroom activities
- Teacher directed tasks designed to identify specific strengths and weaknesses, e.g. a passage of writing to assess proof-reading skills, a written retell to assess use of conventions.
- Teacher–child interview or conferences designed to focus on what children understand and how they use writing skills and strategies.
- Questionnaires, attitude to writing surveys, interest inventories.
- Use of children's self-evaluation comments or checklists.
- Use of teacher made checklists or published diagnostic tests.

To gather specific information about children's writing, teachers may choose some of the following suggestions:

Knowledge and Understandings

(Content, Organisation and Contextual Understandings; Language Concepts and Conventions; Word Usage)

- Observation of children during free choice, diary or journal writing sessions
- Analysis of a range of writing in specific subject areas, e.g. Science Report, Social Studies Explanation
- Writing logs that record of range and type of writing completed
- Written retells
- Checklists, e.g. alphabet knowledge, concepts of print
- Analysis of any draft writing to assess range of vocabulary used
- Analysis of any draft writing to assess spelling strategies used
- Observation of children involved in own or peer editing
- Set texts or passages of published or children's text with errors that children have proof read and revised

Attitudes to Writing

- Interviews / Attitude Surveys / Goals
- Conferences
- Children's written reflections in journals
- Children's self evaluation

Strategies

(planning, organising and revising writing)

- Observation of spelling strategies used in have-a-go pads or other written work
- Observation of children's strategies before, during and after writing
- Analysis of plans for writing
- Observation of note taking
- Interviews with children about their strategies for planning writing
- Interviews with children about their strategies for revising writing

Step 2
Plot the Child on the *Writing: Developmental Continuum*

Focus on the key indicators to determine the phase. Mark all indicators exhibited.

Step 3
Analyse the Indicators Marked

Determine which key indicators need to be developed. Read the *Major Teaching Emphases* for the child's phase.

The *Writing: Developmental Continuum* is designed to use this information to diagnose specific strengths and weaknesses. Many suggestions for intervention at each phase are included in that book. Check to see that these ideas have been tried at the appropriate developmental level.

Step 4
Plan an Intervention Program

Focus on one particular aspect of writing and use ideas from *Writing: Developmental Continuum* and *Writing: Resource Book* to help plan a program in which the child's needs will be met during whole class, small group or individual activities.

Step 5
Organise a Parent-Teacher Conference

Ask parents to talk about their child's writing at home. Use the *Writing: Developmental Continuum* to explain how their child's writing is developing. Show any samples of writing. Give parents information about helping their child's writing.

Step 6
Implement Plans

Begin with a teacher-child meeting. Discuss how the child can set and monitor own goals and start a writing journal.

Step 7
Monitor Continuously

Continue to observe child's writing development and gather information about strategies, interests and attitudes.

Step 8
Plot the Child on the *Writing: Developmental Continuum*

After about a month, mark indicators on the *Writing: Developmental Continuum*. Analyse information.

Step 9
Review Plans

Examine existing plans and refine or alter to ensure identified needs are being met.

Ideas to Include in an Intervention Program

Suggestions to Build Knowledge and Understanding About Writing

(Content, Organisation and Contextual Understandings;
Language Concepts and Conventions; Word Usage)

Planning to get more time

Students will absorb much information in the whole class setting. Small group instruction may follow such sessions to allow teachers to focus on particular needs of children, e.g. brainstorming followed by small group instruction to sort and classify information while remainder of class work independently on that task.

Teacher modelling

Teacher modelling of the process of writing provides children with an insight into the sort of thinking that goes on when people write. To some children this is enlightening because they believe that they are the only person in the world who can't write. When they see a trusted adult tussling with topic selection, rewriting parts of a sentence, looking for the right words, checking spelling or revising and changing writing they realise that writing is do-able. This knowledge gives them confidence to try.

Modelled writing can also be used to teach a particular element in language. For example, if a number of children were beginning to use speech marks, then it would be appropriate for the teacher to model a piece of writing using speech marks and talk about where they go and why. If some children were writing short, repetitive sentences that tended to begin with 'Then...', it would be useful to model sentence-combining techniques.

Modelled writing assists children to:

- identify the specific elements of a convention or form
- critically appraise their own writing
- take responsibility for proof reading
- conduct focused and relevant peer conferences
- help each other with the writing process

Writing for fun

Not all writing should have to be a grand masterpiece. Some children who are seen to be having difficulties are just turned off by writing. Consider some of the following and encourage all children to engage in fun writing:

Letters – personal, to thank, to invite
Notes – to remind, to a classmate, to record information, to the teacher
Posters, advertisements, signs
Limericks, songs and rhymes
Memos and messages
Lists
Greeting cards of all sorts

Modelling different forms

The following modelled writing suggestions will help reluctant writers see that writing can be fun as children join in with the writing process. It is important not to demonstrate too many strategies in any one session.

- Model a simple letter or note. Read and re-read as the writing of the letter progresses. If some children are beginning to use full stops in their writing the teacher might focus on this convention:

That's the end of my idea so I'd better put a full stop there.

The letter or note could be re-read the next day and used as a basis for a phonics lesson.
- Draw an illustrated and labelled map relating to a current class topic, e.g. pirates, a garden with a snail trail.
- Model a simple report, e.g. of a class visit.

Simple patterns

- Present a simple pattern: I like… but I hate…
(While modelling, demonstrate how you are thinking and making decisions as the author.)

I like cats, but I hate sneezing.
I like dogs, but I hate getting licked.
I like camping, but I hate mosquitoes.
I like swimming, but I hate water going up my nose.
I like cooking, but I hate clearing up. (I'll change this to *cleaning up*)
I like sweets, but I hate boiled cabbage.   (I'll change this to *rice pudding*)
I like hot weather, but I hate cold weather. (I'll edit this one to make it more interesting),

e.g. *I like summer rain, but I hate the drizzle of winter.*

- Draw children's attention to the links between ideas, e.g.

*I like **cats**, but I hate **sneezing**.*
*I like **dogs**, but I hate **being licked**.*
Cats and sneezing go together, as do dogs and being licked.

Alphabet activities

- List the letters of the alphabet vertically:

A

B

C

D

- Brainstorm a range of adjectives and people:
Fill them in as you think of them—don't attempt
to go through the alphabet in order.

awful, angry	A	acrobats
bad, bold, big	B	
	C	carpenters
dotty	D	doctors, dentists
	E	engine drivers
fat	F	
	G	grocers

- Work on filling the gaps.
- Choose the best adjectives for each person.

Now let the children try in pairs or groups, with animals. Help them with difficult letters (I, J, U, V, etc.). Let them know that it is sometimes necessary to 'cheat' on difficult letters such as 'x'.

Awful Animals

angry ants	*naughty newts*
beautiful bats	*outrageous orang-utans*
creeping cats	*peculiar possums*
dumb dogs	*queer quokkas*
enormous elephants	*rude rats*
fat fleas	*slithery snakes*
green giraffes	*teeny tadpoles*
huge hippos	*ugly unicorns*
impossible ibises	*vicious vultures*
jolly jumbucks	*willing whales*
keen kangaroos	*excellent oxen*
large lambs	*young yaks*
magic mice	*zany zebras*

- Have the children illustrate the alphabet.
- Make it into a frieze or book.

Lists

Five Reasons For Banning Watermelons

(While modelling, continue to demonstrate how you are thinking and making decisions as the author.)

Watermelons should be banned because:
- *the juice trickles down my arms/elbows.*
- *my _ get sticky when I'm eating a big slice.* (I'll leave out a word and add it in later.)
- *my grandma told me that if I swallow a seed, a watermelon plant will grow inside me.*
  (I'll edit to *out of my ears.*)
- *my sister always beats me in a seed-spitting competition.*
- *it makes me burp.* (I'll edit *it* to *they make.*)
- *Mum gets cranky if I eat watermelon inside the house.*

Talk about this kind of list and how it can be arranged.

Discuss what the children could write about—it doesn't have to be food.

- Six Things I Should Definitely Not Tell My Mother
  I should NOT tell my mother:
  - *that my pet snake has escaped;*
  - *that I crawled under my bed and found a piece of last summer's rock melon;*
  - *that there's a slug in her salad roll (change to half a slug);*
  - *the baby just ate a dead cockroach;* and
  - *that I taped over her favourite video.*
  (The focus here could be on punctuation for lists and getting the twist into the writing. This topic is probably suited to older children as young children have difficulty because of the negative connotations.)

String writing
- Choose a person or animal, e.g. *children.*
- Brainstorm what they are doing and where they might be doing it.

tripping	bathroom
crashing	stair
yelling	kitchen
groaning	garden
puffing	sea
chewing	paddock
splashing	tree

- Re-arrange and match the action and location, using the initial letters where possible. Add any more as they come to you—put a catchy line that rhymes at end of each verse, e.g.

  Crashing in the kitchen,
  Splashing in the sea,
  Yelling in the backyard-
  Can't catch me!
  Puffing in the paddock,
  Slipping on the stair,
  Chewing all the lamb chops-
  That's not fair!
  Bawling in the bathroom,

Tripping by the tree,
Groaning in the garden-
Poor old me!

- Now brainstorm words for another subject such as a puppy—and let the children try.

chewing	rubbish bin
chasing	kitchen
licking	sofa
rolling	flower bed
scratching	beach

Riddles

- Read one with the children.
  Clue: **It's got four legs**.

My first is in *dog* but not in *log*.
My second is in the letter between '*h*' and '*j*'.
My third is in *bang* but not in *bag*.
My fourth is in *green* and *magic* and *huge*.
My fifth is a vowel in *owl*.
My whole is something that howls in the night.
Answer: DINGO

Discuss the different clues, e.g.
Line one—only one letter is different
Line two—a good stop-gap
Line three—there is only one extra letter added
Line four—only one letter in common
Line five—could have been the first vowel in *outside*, or the second vowel in *below*, etc.

- Now model the writing of one with the children.
  Clue: **It can swim like a fish**.

My first is in *door* but not in *floor*.
My second is in *octopus* and *orange* and *out*.
My third is in *late* but not in *gate*.
My fourth is in the letter after '*N*' and before '*Q*'.
My fifth is the second letter in *this*.
My sixth is in *prick* and also in *fig*.
My seventh is the fourteenth letter of the alphabet.
My whole is something that swims in the sea.
Answer: DOLPHIN

As you model try different words and discard them, alter clues, cross out, etc.

Descriptions

- Choose someone in the school. The teacher writes a *Who Am I?* description and children try to guess who it is. Describe: physical attributes, job, hobbies, pet hates. Save a final identifying attribute till last. Have the children analyse the description framework. Talk about the need to plan and write descriptions in paragraphs.
  Note: When modelling a *Who Am I?* description, discuss the importance of leaving the key identifying features until last.

Limericks

- Read a limerick:
  There was a young donkey called Fred,
  Who wanted to sleep in a bed.
  He was terribly fat
  And he squashed it quite flat—
  So he slept in a paddock instead!

- Discuss rhyme, rhythm and structure. Model the writing of a limerick:
  - Decide on a topic—Three Springs Primary School
    There is a great school at Three Springs
  - What rhymes with springs? Go through the alphabet:

brings	*wings*
flings	*clings*
rings	*kings*
things	*sings*

  - Pick on a possible word and see if it works—*kings.*
    Where the students are happy as kings.
  - Possible next line—*They're all very clever*

  Discard, because nothing that rhymes with *clever* seems to work, e.g. *never, sever.*
  - Try again—*At sport they are good*—discard for same reason.
  - Try again—*At work they excel*

bell	*dell*	
fell	*sell*	*shell*
tell	*well*	

    And they're sporty as well
  - Go back to first list:
    They can run like a lizard with wings.
  - Final version
    There is a great school at Three Springs,
    Where the students are happy as kings.
    At work they excel,
    They are sporty as well—
    They can run like a lizard with wings!

- Model another limerick with the children before they write their own. Use the same process, but introduce a way to cheat if you can't get the rhymes to work—e.g. inventing a name:
  There once was a tom cat called Gnaws,
  Who had the most ginormous claws.
  (gigantic-enormous)
  When he turned round and round,
  He made holes in the ground—
  So he had to wear gloves on his paws!

Skeleton outlines and semantic grids

1 Give the students a short text relating to a theme such as 'animals', e.g. an extract from a book (approximately two paragraphs), or an extract from a children's encyclopedia.
2 With the children create a skeleton outline (see Sample A).
3 Give the students another text on the same topic and let them create their own skeleton outline, using the same headings. The result might be like Sample B.

4 Have the children research another item in the same area. Encourage them to write a skeleton outline (as in Samples C and D).
5 Jointly construct a text and have children write a short text using their own skeleton outline as a framework.
6 With the students, transfer information from the skeleton outlines onto a semantic grid.
7 Synthesise information noted on the semantic grid—generalise, infer, etc.

SAMPLE A: BROWN BEARS
Habitat
Most in Europe, North America
Some in Asia, South America

Size
Height 3.4 metres
Weight 750 kilograms

Food
Fish
Other animals

Interesting features
Poor eyesight
Good sense of smell
Sleep all winter
Run at 50 km per hour

SAMPLE B: WALRUSES
Habitat
Only in freezing Arctic waters near Canada,
Alaska, Russia, Scandinavia

Size
Length 4.5 metres
Weight 360 kilograms

Food
Clams
Fish
Seals

Interesting features
Ivory tusks
Feet like fins
Live in the sea most of the time
Have 15 cm of blubber to keep them warm
Ride on ice floes

SAMPLE C: EMUS
Habitat
Australia

Size
The second largest bird in the world
Height 2 metres
Weight 36-37 kg

Food
Grass, berries, insects, fruit

Interesting features
Cannot fly
Can run at 50 km per hour
Strides 4 metres long

SAMPLE D: RHINOS
Habitat
Asia, India, Africa

Size
The second largest animal that lives on land
Weight $\frac{1}{2}$–$1\frac{1}{2}$ tonnes

Food
Grass $\frac{1}{2}$ tonne a day
trees, shrubs

Interesting features
African rhinos have two horns
Asian rhinos have one horn
The horns are 1.65 metres long
Rhinos wallow in mud to get rid of insects and to keep cool.
Tick-birds and rhinos help each other.
Rhinos give tick-birds a home.
Tick-birds eat annoying insects and warn rhinos of danger

Semantic Grid

Name	Habitat	Size	Food	Interesting Features
Brown Bear				
Walrus				
Emu				
Rhino				

This activity can be modified to meet the needs of a wide range of children in a class, provided that all the children have learned about skeleton outlines, for example,

Group A   -   Give children the texts and completed skeleton outlines. Ask them to mark the relevant information in the texts with highlighter pens.

Group B   -   Give children the texts and an 'empty' skeleton outline. Ask the children to find the relevant information in the text and fill in the outline.

Group C   -   Give the children the texts and ask them to construct a skeleton outline independently.

It will be found that all the children complete their tasks at about the same time. All will have gained a further understanding of the content and of processes involved in composition. The teacher will have been able to cater for a range of abilities.

Serial writing

When modelling a long piece of writing, it is useful to write a section at a time over several days. The section can be written in front of the children, or displayed earlier, then edited and proof read while the children watch.

When editing, train children to ask the types of questions that will help them when editing their writing with partners. Questions should focus on clarifying the writing, e.g. *When did this happen?*, *What exactly do you mean?* etc. Have children suggest alternatives as you focus on making the writing more interesting. Read and re-read as you clarify your thoughts on the writing. This is a useful time to focus on punctuation, grammatical features, sentence combining, etc.

Joint construction

Joint construction of texts involves the teacher and children or children in pairs or small groups working collaboratively to produce a written text. Children are able to participate in the successful writing of a complete text and gain confidence from this experience.

Guided writing

Guided writing occurs when the student has time to write and the teacher is available to give guidance. It follows many demonstrations by the teacher and provides a bridge to independent writing for children who lack the confidence to try on their own. This may occur with individuals or small groups. The teacher supports and extends the thinking of the writers to help them control the form, style, or clarity of the writing. The writer retains control of the writing while the teacher acts as a facilitator. It is a strategy that builds confidence.

Real writing

The subject matter of writing is best generated from children's personal, social and educational needs, experiences and interests. Children need something to write about. Sometimes children who are having difficulties with writing feel that they have nothing to write about. Provision of shared classroom experiences helps to build confidence in these children as they have a common starting point and feel that they have ideas to contribute. They also have sufficient relevant vocabulary having talked freely with others to clarify and order their ideas. Experiences may be excursions out of the classroom or 'hands on' activities such as maths or science investigations.

Areas such as Social Studies, Science and Health provide a range of information which will provide the basis of many language opportunities. Teachers need to plan a flexible program to enable those children having difficulties to have some choices in what they write so that they have sufficient interest and information to complete the task, e.g. after making an item in craft time children could write the instructions for others to make the same thing or make notes and explain on tape how the article was made. (Procedure)

Investigate the local community. Involve children in noting the features of the area and services provided. Compile the information and give it to new families arriving in the area. (Report)

Provide classroom and outside experiences for children to talk about and draw writing from these experiences, e.g. How I Solved the Maths Problem (Recount).

Encourage children to develop logical arguments to support their point of view about issues that affect them and invite them to use writing to influence others (letters to relevant authorities—Expositions).

Move from the known to unknown

As children write in different areas of the curriculum for different purposes they will gain confidence and essential practice in a range of different forms. By allowing time for children to clarify existing knowledge and then to set their own questions, children are likely to feel more able and willing to focus their writing. Children could:

- brainstorm to activate background knowledge in Social Studies or Science
- categorise information to direct their notetaking
- before starting a new topic make a 'Things I want to know' list
- make a 'Things I now know' list after completing a topic

Print experiences

Children's experiences of print will have a profound effect on the writing produced. Stories, poems, expository texts, songs and jingles all serve as models for children's writing. They influence what is written and how it is written. Teachers therefore need to read to children and allow children to have access to a range of meaningful texts for independent reading. Children will benefit from repeated readings of their favourite texts and meaningful and purposeful experiences with print will help children learn to write.

Dictate onto audio tape

Encourage students to use tape recording as a means of capturing their ideas. Tapes can be transcribed by willing helpers and made into books for children to read.

Story tapes

Give older children a reason to write stories by asking them to read their own stories onto tape and make taped books for younger children to read.

Written conversations

Start a written conversation with a child. An open ended question is often a good starter, e.g. What do you think about the...? Encourage the child to write an answer and keep the conversation going. Try to include words they have misspelt and model the correct spelling in the answer.

Rebus writing

Model the use of pictures to substitute for words and ask students to write their own rebuses for others to decode.

Text innovation

Text innovation involves children in using familiar text structures as frameworks for their own writing. This kind of support enables children who are having difficulties with writing to have success as they compose their own versions. Children may innovate on a text structure by:

- changing words or phrases
- changing characters
- adding or deleting characters
- changing settings
- extending stories
- changing beginnings or endings
- substituting antonyms for all adjectives

Suggestions to Build the Belief that Everyone Can Write
(Attitude)

The teacher's role

The teacher's role is to foster children's willingness to write. This can be done by talking to children, individually, about their feelings regarding writing. Teachers can share their own feelings, successes and problems experienced when writing and assure children that if they know how to talk they will be able to learn how to write. Children must share the belief that they can write and teachers must trust that they will.

Provide authentic purposes and audiences. Many children who have writing difficulties believe that the only purpose for writing is to get a 'good' mark and as they believe they can't do that, they are unlikely to try. These children need to be engaged in writing that is relevant to them and to see that writing can be for different audiences ranging from oneself to a whole group of people.

Much writing which is done in schools is to demonstrate the ability to write. The teacher's role of judge conflicts with the role of audience, so if other audiences can be found the teacher can be freed to act as a co-writer working with the writer to create effective writing for 'real' audiences. Even experienced writers have difficulty writing if they are unsure of the purpose and audience for writing. These two aspects are central to writing yet often difficult to replicate in classrooms. All writing must be shaped by its purpose and audience.

Audiences for young writers must be concrete and immediate so sharing time is critical to young writers. The classroom provides a real audience but the climate must be supportive and secure so that writers who are having difficulties can feel safe to share their efforts. Teacher modelling of appropriate audience reaction and requirements for participation is critical to this process.

Message boards

Start a message board in the classroom. (A large piece of laminated card can be re-used many times.) The teacher and children are all encouraged to write messages. Read the messages daily and make sure that the students see the value of writing them.

Sharing circle

Children are encouraged to join a sharing circle where they can discuss their writing problems or identify pleasing aspects of their work. They need explicit guidance in the conduct of these sessions. The group sits in a circle and one child reads the writing aloud, other group members listen and give feedback or ask questions. Alternatively, the child reads part of the text and asks for comments or suggestions for improvement. When all children have had an opportunity to give feedback the writer then tells the group what decisions he/she has made about the writing. Other group members proceed in the same manner.

It can be useful at times to have a focus for the sharing session, e.g. 'This week we are concentrating on great descriptions. Let's all see how we can paint a word picture for our audience.' In this way all children can concentrate on one small aspect of writing. Sharing circles can also be used for peer editing where children check each other's work using a checklist of items to be examined.

Tips for writers

Teachers can do much to help children believe they can write. The following suggestions are easily passed on to children and will help them understand that writing is not always a grand production but can start from small, personal things.

Children can:

- carry a small notebook to record things seen. (Notebooks are personal but should be used each day)
- record feelings
- read a lot and jot down anything that appeals
- write down any tips people give for writing
- write tips that they use and share them with others

Focus on strengths

When focusing on children's writing it is important to respond to the message in the print first, e.g. 'You know a lot about frogs '. Only after responding to the message is it appropriate for teachers to direct attention to a specific skill or area for improvement if necessary. Often it is useful to ask the child in which area he/she thinks help is needed. Students who are having difficulties can probably only attend to one area at a time or to one part of a whole text. It is far better to provide a narrow focus first so that the text does not end up with masses of red marks and the child is not daunted by the enormity of the task. Some teachers have encouraged children by making suggestions on post-it stickers or by photocopying the child's writing so that corrections can be made on the copy leaving the original intact. These actions have shown writers that the teacher respects the ownership of the writing.

The environment

The class environment must be one where risk-taking and experimenting with writing are supported and approximations are valued. There should be a feeling that this is a community of writers and readers who all support each other.

Free writing

Setting aside time for children to write freely without having to worry about corrections or other audiences may be a way of encouraging writers to have-a-go and play around with writing. This writing can be in the form of notes, diary entries or journals which teachers are invited to read. The activity could be continued until children write freely without inhibition.

Speed writing

Invite children to engage in speed writing each day. Children may talk about what they will write for two minutes before they start. Allow five minutes and ask children to see how many words they can write. Words must be able to be read by another person.

Writing journals

A writing journal provides students with an opportunity to reflect upon their progress as writers. Before beginning, teachers can model the use of journals and share their own entries with children. A writing journal could include:

- personal goals for writing
- lists of texts written
- thoughts about writing
- personal reports about their writing—I think I am a ....writer because...
- words, and phrases that may be included in writing later
- drawings of things that may be included in writing
- suggestions made by the teacher or peers to improve writing
- comments or reflections about books read.

Suggestions to Develop Children's Strategies to Use Before, During and After Writing

Teachers need to be explicit about the writing processes used before, during and after writing. Children with writing problems need many opportunities to practise all strategies.

Choosing topics and getting started

This is often a problem with children who are having difficulties with writing.

- Show children how to brainstorm. Start with general topics and show how you move to specifics, e.g. Celebrations… Birthdays… My Worst Birthday
- Show how to move from talking to writing by jotting ideas to do with the topic on small pieces of paper and then arranging these on a single sheet in some sort of order. Add any other ideas.
- Show how to start a 'Possibles' list of topics for another time
- Develop an interest in playing with words
- Show that it is common for writers to make false starts

Reading as a writer

During shared reading sessions encourage children to think about things the author has done to make the text effective. Ask questions, e.g.

What did the author have to know to write this text?
How did the author make you want to read on?
Why do you think the author included that piece of information?
What might the author make happen next? Why do you think that?
If you were the author how would this story end? Why?
How does the author make you feel about the main character?

Use planning frameworks

Show children how to use the various planning frameworks to organise their writing. These frameworks are not meant to be used as a recipe for writing, but they do support children as they begin to learn to write in different contexts. Children having difficulties may need to use them to reduce the load on their working memory so they can concentrate on other aspects of writing.

Use available resources

Teachers can model the way they use a range of resources such as word banks, dictionaries or thesauruses and other resources to show students that the use of these resources helps to enhance their writing. Thesaurus and dictionary games help children to develop understanding about the words they use and the way to locate them.

Spelling aids

If children are severely hampered by poor spelling, encourage the use of a range of strategies including the use of computer spell checks and phonetic dictionaries.

Encourage risk taking

Modelling how to attempt the spelling of new words provides children with ideas they can use themselves. Many reluctant writers are unwilling to try to spell new words because they fear the ramifications of getting them wrong. Talking about ways to deal with this problem will give students a chance to experience the freedom of trying out new words to enhance their writing. Charts such as the one below can be jointly constructed so that students feel that the ideas represented are their ideas.

How do I spell a new word?

Use a 'Have-a-go' card

- Think about meaning. Does it give any clues to spelling patterns?

- Say the word slowly. Listen carefully.

- Write the word syllable by syllable.

- Make sure you have represented each sound with a letter or letters.

- Look carefully to see if the pattern
- Looks right, if not:

   – Try different patterns that might be right

   – See if you know another word which is similar

Personal word lists

Encouraging children to build up personal word lists that can be used as a reference is one way of getting children to take responsibility for their own spelling. In addition to this, students who are having difficulties with writing need strategies to help them learn to spell new words they wish to use in their writing. The Look, Say, Cover, Write, Check method is one way of getting children to focus on the part of the word which is causing them trouble.

Editing help

Peer editing, oral editing, group composition, group conferences; discussion groups and partner work can all be used to help writers improve their writing

Teaching proof reading

Explicit teaching of ways to proof read text is an essential part of helping children who have writing difficulties. Work with children to establish proof-reading guidelines. (Don't impose editing on struggling writers—it is better to get them writing fluently first.)

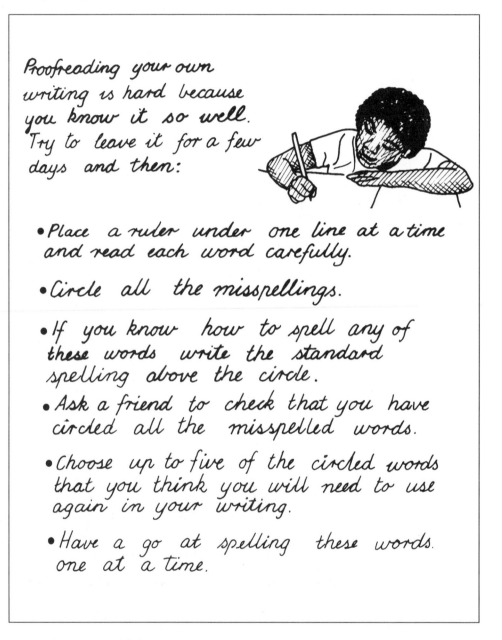

Proofreading your own writing is hard because you know it so well. Try to leave it for a few days and then:

- Place a ruler under one line at a time and read each word carefully.

- Circle all the misspellings.

- If you know how to spell any of these words write the standard spelling above the circle.

- Ask a friend to check that you have circled all the misspelled words.

- Choose up to five of the circled words that you think you will need to use again in your writing.

- Have a go at spelling these words one at a time.

Remember every child can write.

INTERVENTION PLAN	Whole class	Small group	Individual
Name: _____ Birthdate: _____ Date: _____			
Key writing strategies to be encouraged:			
Developing knowledge and understanding			
Strategies to develop a positive attitude			
Strategies for planning, organising and revising writing			

APPENDIX – Forms of Writing Checklist

Use the checklists below and on the following page to indicate where different forms of writing are modelled and introduced across the curriculum. Use the checklists for planning or recording topics.

FORMS OF WRITING

Checklist   **term** [ ]

FORMS OF TEXT	SOCIAL STUDIES	SCIENCE	HEALTH	MATHS	OTHER

Informational
  Recount
  Procedures
  Explanations					

Descriptions					
Reports					
Summaries					
Notes					
Expositions and Debates					
Interviews					
Instructions					
Letters **- Personal** **- Formal**					
Invitations					
Greetings					

FORMS OF TEXT	SOCIAL STUDIES	SCIENCE	HEALTH	MATHS	OTHER
Figures: • graphs • tables • diagrams • charts					
Maps					
Timetables					
Advertisements					
Narrative					
Anecdotes					
Fiction					
Traditional Tales: • fairy tales • folk tales • fables					
Myths and legends					
Fantasy and Science Fiction					
Poetic					

Acknowledgements

We gratefully acknowledge the work of :

Glenda Raison, Education Officer, First Steps Project, Ministry of Education and Judith Rivalland, Senior Lecturer in Communications Education, Edith Cowan University for the Assessment and Evaluation sections from The Writing Learning Continuum

Beverly Derewianka, Lecturer in Language Education at the University of Wollongong

Dr Peter Sloan and Dr Ross Latham, Edith Cowan University, Perth , Western Australia for sections from Teaching Children How to Write Informational Texts written for the First Steps Project

Terry D. Johnson, Professor of Education, Faculty of Education, University of Victoria, British Columbia, Canada and Kay Kovalevs, Christmas Island District High School for sections from A Problem Solving Approach to Teaching Writing Module

Ross Bindon, Bunbury District Education Office for information from the Teaching Grammar Module

Alison Dewsbury, Kevlynn Annandale and Judith Larsen for sections from the Modelled Writing Module

Kay Kovalevs for her dedication and hard work in the editing and co-ordination of the First Steps books in the early years of the project. She also contributed to and collated the ESL research into children's language learning at Christmas Island District High School

Bibliography

Alford P. (n.d.) *Written English Programme*, Upper Great Southern Regional Office, Narrogin, WA.

Bean W. & Bouffler C. 1986, *Spell by Writing*, Primary English Teaching Association (PETA), Rozelle, NSW.

Brown H. & Cambourne B. 1987, *Read and Retell*, Thomas Nelson, Melbourne.

Butler A. & Turbill J. 1984, *Towards a Reading, Writing Classroom*, Primary English Teaching Association (PETA), Rozelle, NSW.

Cambourne B. & Turbill J. 1987, *Coping with Chaos*, Primary English Teaching Association (PETA), Rozelle, NSW.

Cambourne B. 1988, *The Whole Story*, Ashton Scholastic, Auckland, NZ.

Christie F. & Rothery J. 1989, *Writing in Schools, Reader*, Deakin University Press, Geelong, VIC.

Clutterbuck P. 1989, *The Art of Teaching Grammar,* Longman Cheshire, Melbourne.

Collerson J. 1988, *Writing for Life*, Primary English Teaching Association (PETA), Rozelle, NSW.

Curriculum Branch 1985, *Programming Ideas K–7*, Vol. 5, Education Department of WA, Perth.

Curriculum Branch 1982, *Social Studies Teachers Guides K–7*, Education Department of Western Australia, Perth.

Curriculum Branch 1983, *Reading K–7 Teachers Notes*, Education Department of Western Australia, Perth.

Curriculum Branch 1986, *Writing K–7 Teachers Notes*, Education Department of Western Australia, Perth.

Curriculum Branch, *Speaking and Listening K–7 Teachers Notes*, (Draft Ed.), Education Department of Western Australia, Perth.

Curriculum Branch 1989, *K-7 English Language Syllabus,* Ministry of Education, Perth, WA.

Derewianka B. 1990, *Exploring How Texts Work*, Primary English Teaching Association (PETA), Rozelle, NSW.

ECT 418 Language Studies Children's Writing 1984, *Children's Writing: Study Guide*, Deakin University Press, Geelong, VIC.

Frank M. 1979, *If you're trying to teach kids to write, you've just gotta have this book*, Incentive Publications, Nashville, Tennessee, USA.

Graves, D.H. 1981, *Writing: Teachers and Children at Work*, Heinemann Educational, Melbourne.

Greg L.W. & Steinberg I.R. 1980, *Cognitive Processes in Writing*, Lawrence Earlbaum Association, New Jersey, USA.

Heenan J.E. 1986, *Writing Process and Product*, Longman Paul Ltd, Auckland, NZ.

Hillocks, G. 1986, 'Research written composition: new directions for teaching', National Conference on Research in English. *ERIC Clearing House on Reading and Communication Skills*. Urbana, Illinois: National Institute of Education. Quoted in Johnson, Terry D. (1988), *Unriddling the World*, pp. 22, 24. 1986

Howard P. 1986, *Perfect Your Grammar*, Longman Cheshire, Melbourne.

Howard P 1986,. *Perfect Your Punctuation*, Longman Cheshire, Melbourne.

Howard P. 1986, *Perfect Your Sentences*, Longman Cheshire, Melbourne.

Johnston T.D. & Louis D.R. 1985, *Literacy Through Literature*, Methuen Australia, Melbourne.

Johnston T.D. 1988, *Unriddling the World*, Wesley Foundation for Research in Literacy Inc., South Perth.

Kroll B.M. & Wells G. 1983, *Explorations in the Development of Writing Theory, Research and Practice*, Wiley, Chichester, UK.

Larson R.L. 1975, *Children and Writing in the Elementary School: Theories and Techniques*, Oxford University Press, Oxford, UK.

Martin J.R. 1989, *Technically and Abstraction: Language for Creation of Specialised Knowledge*, Paper presented to Language in Education Conference, Macquarie University, NSW.

Martin J.R. & Rothery J. 1988, *Classification and Framing: Double Dealing in a Pedagogic Discourse*, Paper presented to Post-World Reading Symposium: Language in Learning, University of Sydney, NSW.

Martin J.R. & Rothery J. 1986, *Exploring and Explaining: Factual Writing in the Primary School*, Paper presented to ARA Conference, Perth, WA.

Martin J.R., and Rothery, Joan 1986, 'Writing report project': *Working Papers in Linguistics* No 4, Linguistics Department, University of Sydney, NSW.

McCracken M.A. & McCracken R.J. 1979, *Reading, Writing and Language: A Practical Guide for Primary Teachers*, Peguis, Winnipeg, CANADA.

Moffatt, James 1965, *College Composition and Communicating*, No. 16, 5 December, pp, 243–48. Quoted in Johnson, Terry D. (1988) *Unriddling the World*, p. 44, 1988

Research Branch (unpub.) Writing Profiles, Education Department of Western Australia, Perth.

Roberts V. 1985, *Conferencing with Confidence*, PETA PEN Note No.53, PETA, Rozelle, NSW. 1985

Sager, C. 'Improving the Quality of Written Composition by Pupil Use of Rating Scales'. Paper presented to the Annual Meeting of NECTE. ERIC ED 089 304, Washington, D.C. 1973 Quoted in Johnson, Terry D. *Unriddling the World*, p. 22, 1988

Sloan P. & Latham R. 1989, *Teaching Frameworks*, Paper presented to ARA Conference, Perth.

Temple C.A., Nathan R.G. & Burns N.A. 1982, *The Beginnings of Writing*, Allyn & Bacon Inc., Boston, Massachusetts, USA.

Wilkinson A., Barnsley G., Hanna P. & Swan M. 1980, *Assessing Language Development*, Oxford University Press, Oxford, UK.